Near/Miss

Near/Miss

CHARLES BERNSTEIN

The University of Chicago Press

Chicago and London

The University of Chicago Press, Chicago 60637
The University of Chicago Press, Ltd., London
© 2018 by Charles Bernstein.
Published 2018
Printed in the United States of America

27 26 25 24 23 22 21 20 19 18   1 2 3 4 5

ISBN-13: 978-0-226-57072-3 (cloth)
ISBN-13: 978-0-226-57069-3 (paper)
ISBN-13: 978-0-226-57119-5 (e-book)
DOI: https://doi.org/10.7208/chicago/9780226571195.001.0001

Library of Congress Cataloging-in-Publication Data

Names: Bernstein, Charles, 1950– author.
Title: Near/miss / Charles Bernstein.
Description: Chicago ; London : The University of Chicago
    Press, 2018.
Identifiers: LCCN 2018002466 | ISBN 9780226570723 (cloth :
    alk. paper) | ISBN 9780226570693 (pbk. : alk. paper) | ISBN
    9780226571195 (e-book)
Classification: LCC PS3552.E7327 N437 2018 | DDC 811/.54—
    dc23
LC record available at https://lccn.loc.gov/2018002466

♾ This paper meets the requirements of ANSI/NISO
Z39.48-1992 (Permanence of Paper).

CONTENTS

Near/Miss

Un bateau frêle comme un papillon de mai.

This is a totally
inaccessible poem.
Each word,
phrase &
line
has been de-
signed to puz-
zle you, its
read-
er, & to
test whether
you're intel-
lect-
ual enough—
well-read or dis-
cern-
ing e-
nough—to ful-
ly appreciate th-
is
poem. This poem
has been written
for an audience of
poets, poets
who know the dif-
ference be-
tween the
simple past

tense & 'has
been'—the pres-
ent per-
fect tense
—&
who also rec-
ognize the pos-
sible aesthetic
effect of that dif-
ference—poets
who also know
that 'has been' has
another meaning
even though that
other meaning is
not relevant to
this poem. This
poem
is un-
necessarily com-
plicated,
flailing wild-
ly, like an
opium addict looking
vainly for its
pipe, at a
demo-
nstrably deranged
a-
version of the necessary
in quest of
the im-
probable (necessity
is to this
poem what mar-
garine is to marzi-

pan).
This
poem cries
out for an audience
that is able
to savor
the use of
a
sing-
le quo-
tation mark
where
less sens-
i-
tive read-
ers would
fail to see
why double
quotes were-
n't used &
might
even be so fool-
ish to think
that using sin-
gle quotes was
a mis-
take or pre-
tenti-
ous. This
poem has been
written not for
just any other
poets
but for
those
special ones

capable
of appreciating the
nu-
ances &
tricks, pros-
oody &
infrastruct-
ures (or
their
ab-
sence) in
this poem. This
poem
fancies poetry
as an ei-
detic
emanation
so rare & so
refined
that it will
e-
lude
even the m-
ost elite
readers, which
almost certain-
ly
does not
(& will
never)
in-
clude
you.
Its
attitude
toward you

as a
g-
eneral reader
is that
you'd
be better off
watching BBC news
or listen-
ing
to NPR human-
interest program-
ming
or, anyway,
stick-
ing to
the laur-
e-
ates. This
poem
appeals to
a small co-
ter-
ie of those
in the k-
now
by making
in-group references
that will leave you
scratch-
ing your
head (if your hand
ever
frees it-
self from scratch-
ing your
ass). This

poem is laced—
as tea is
laced
with arsenic
but also as
lace is made in
Chantilly—
with coded winks
to béret-clad
cogno-
scenti,
sly references
such as
the fact that
the title
of this poem
refers to another
poem,
which is n-
ever
referenced
in this poem,
or not
referenced in
a way the
broad public would be
hip en-
ough to be
hip to—(
dig it?)
—
so, heh!,
if
you're not
hip to
that oth-

er poem
you will be
as out to sea
with this
poem as
the proverb-
ial organ grind-
er who
lost his monkey—
not in the great
storm raging (al-
ways rag-
ing) out-
side, but in
the head-
ier storm raging—
raging like a god
who's lost his
sheep or a
mil-
linery salesman
who's lost his
samples—
in the supernal storm
raging inside
the or-
gan grind-
er's mind. &
speaking of the title
of this poem, as we
have been doing
(*we* if, but
only if, you
have—'gainst
all good judgment—
accepted this

poem's in-
souciant so-
licitation)—have
you noticed
(careful readers sure-
ly woulda) that
the title of
this poem seems
to bear
no re-
lation to the
text that
fol-
lows?
This imparts this
poem with an extra
shot of a-
ura, at
least for those
cleverer 'nough
to appreciate the
conceit.
But leaving aside
whether or not
the title is con-
nect-
ed to the
poem, the
title does make
an acute social
ob-
serv-
ation that nowadays
no-
body
wants to accept

gratitude:
they want to bestow it,
but not receive
it. (—
"Thank you
for writing this
poem."—"No,
not at all, I
must thank you
for reading
it.")—This
poem believes
that po-
etry's a high-
er calling. For
this rea-
son, th-
is
poem can't
be both-
ered with the
e-
motions &
cares, trag-
edies & cele-
brations, tor-
ments
& e-
lations, worries &
ministrations, preferences
& aver-
sions, spites
& likes—of or-
dinary people like
you—the
com-

mon man but also
common woman &
child, ir-
regardless
of wheth-
er gay,
straight, mix-
ed or
can't (or
won't or would
pre-
fer not
to) be
cat-
e-
gorized, because
who cares about such
categories except a
bunch of bigots—
& whose business is
it anyway? This
poem
has been forced—
with leaden
heart &
downturned
brow (if
such an ex-
pression of
supervening
regret does not, though
I fear
it
most assuredly
does, lapse
into per-

sonif-

i-

cation) . . . this

poem has

been

forced against its

every aes-

thetic hope,

to turn

its back on

you, the

read-

er, who is,

come on, let's

stop kid-

ding ourselves, a

philistine:

stupid, ig-

nor-

ant &

vulgar, pos-

sessing a limited

vocabulary (if

pos-

sessing any vo-

cabulary at

all & not

simply cruising

it),

a reader who,

mon dieu!,

doesn't

even know

French. This

poem's love is

not the Costco

kind: supersized
& dis-
counted.
It's a tough
love that doesn't
coddle
or treat you like an
idiot
(
even if thou
art
one or
a-
spire to be)
(aesthetic
stu-
pidity is not born
but made
).
A poem is a place to think, not say
As in a game of mouse & cat
Where said & read are both the mouth
Keeping the cat at bay.
—Dearest, most
be-
lovéd
reader (for
despite the
im-
pression I have
hither-
to con-
veyed,
know that you
are al-
ways, & will al-

ways be, fore-
most in my
heart): be-
ware the Dark
Myst-
eries of this
poem, for if, e-
ven for a mo-
ment, you lose
your vigilant
disapprobation
& let the
poem's in-
sidious charms
grab hold of you
by your boot-
straps & shake
you to an inch of your
life—then its
black
magic will fuck
with
your head & comman-
deer
your soul. *Stay calm,*
keep your dis-
tance
& be sure n-
either to cry
n-
or laugh because,
when you do, poetry's
boogeyman will have
trapped you in her
lair—& there's
no known es-

cape
from that (nor
unknown either).
This poem po-
ssesses a near-
ly absolute
know-
ledge—a
virtu-
al-
ly su-
preme truth
that it dis-
closes only
to a bless-
èd
few. This poem's
address
is to E-
ternity
& to those
in the
now
& here—& the
hidden
places in be-
tween—
who chose, of
their own ac-
cord, out
of desire, vision, &
with a leap
of faith border-
ing on
a-
postasy—to

count-
enance & re-
vere it.
It's
unreal.

IN UTOPIA

In utopia they don't got no rules and Prime Minister Cameron's "criminality pure and simple" is reserved for politicians just like him. In utopia the monkey lies down with the rhinoceros and the ghosts haunt the ghosts leaving everyone else to fends for themself. In utopia, you lose the battles and you lose the war too but it bothers you less. In utopia no one tells nobody nothin', but I gotta tell you this. In utopia the plans are ornament and expectations dissolve into whim. In utopia, here is a pivot. In utopia, love goes for the ride but eros's at the wheel. In utopia, the words sing the songs while the singers listen. In utopia, 1 plus 2 does not equal 2 plus 1. In utopia, I and you is not the same as you and me. In utopia, we won't occupy Wall Street, we are Wall Street. In utopia, all that is solid congeals, all that melts liquefies, all that is air vanishes into the late afternoon fog.

HIGH TIDE AT RACE POINT

for Norman Fischer

A commercial with no pitch.
A beach without sand.
A lover without a love.
A surface without an exterior.
A touch without a hand.
A protest without a cause.
A well without a bottom.
A sting without a bite.
A scream without a mouth.
A fist without a fight.
A day without an hour.
A park with no benches.
A poem without a text.
A singer with no voice.
A computer without memory.
A cabana without a beach.
A bump with no road.
A sorrow without a loss.
A goal without a purpose.
A noise without sound.
A story without a plot.
A sail without a boat.
A plane without wings.
A pen without ink.
A murder without a victim.
A sin without a sinner.
An agreement without terms.
A spice with no taste.
A gesture without motion.

A spectator without a view.
A slope without a curve.
A craving without a desire.
A volume without dimension.
A Nazi without a Jew.
A comic without a joke.
A promise without a hope.
A comforter without the comfort.
The certainty without being sure.
Stealing with nothing stolen.
The might have beens without the was.
Mishnah without Torah.
The two without the one.
The silken without the silk.
The inevitable without necessity.
Logic without inference.
Suddenness without change.
A canyon without depth.
Fume without smell.
Determination with no objective.
Gel without cohesion.
A cure without a disease.
A disease without a trace.
A mineral without a shape.
A line without extension.
Persistence without intention.
Blank without emptiness.
Border without division.
A puppet without strings.
Compliance without criteria.
A disappointment without an expectation.
Color without hue.
An idea without content.
Grief with no end.

Of time I can tell you nothing that is
Not already written in sand, scarcely
Noticeable just before the water
Engulfs it without even trace of a
Trace of any inscription remaining.
Man is no better, crumbling in currents
Of perilous recrimination, where
Humanoids dwell in close proximity
To beasts. Who doesn't adore them? It is
The story of the birth of the mother—
Only now I am too paranoid not
To say it in another's words. Or to
Try again, one more time without feeling.
Motion alone encumbers her meaning.

And if in a minute or a few days
The ghost of what is to come
Clatters down on me, pipe in mouth
Or do I claw back to higher ground
Only to be shorn in plain sight
Of nominal excommunications

Rackstraw Downes, *Farm Buildings Near the Rio Grande: Under the Barn Roof, A.M.*, 2008.

NOWHERE IS JUST AROUND THE CORNER

Yeah I know. All that horizontality.
It's enough to drive you to
drink. Vista, schmitza. I just
want a little hope for life, even
if it doesn't pan out. Yeah I
get it: emptiness is plenitude.
At 49.95 a yard. There is nothing
I long for more than a cool,
clear draft of hot air with
geometric framing. The canopy
saves it . . . seriously. A frame
is like a rabbit pulled from a
hat in Dallas, 1948. Baby rabbits
multiplying like Republicans
in Waco trying to shut down
Planned Parenthood as if it were
a tool of Islam. I know Marfa is
not Dallas—but open spaces
seem to translate into open
carry and concealed carry too:
the only adequate response to
gun violence is more gun
violence, isn't that it?,
just like the New York Jew
lawyers say about free

speech. Don't get me wrong:
I love Robert Smithson
& I am all over the spiral
jelly. (Or am I thinking of
Donald Thudd? Association is
like a kaleidoscope of missed
references that form a mosaic
of freighted cymbals.) And don't
get so puffed up: after all Jersey
City is where we are seeing
this painting—and is the local
governor any better than that
Texas governor, I already
forgot his name, Slick Ferry?
Rich Very?, but you know,
the one who ran for president
just like Tricks Christie, governor
of the great state that borders
the Keystone and Empire states,
the state in which we are looking
at this Rackstraw Downes painting?
I mean Rackstraw used to do
New York City scenes until
he got the Marfa bug. The next
thing you know he won't even
paint the ambient structures
but just brush weed. I hope
he has an air-conditioned painting
igloo as I wouldn't like to
see him in pain air, like the
French say, 110 in the shade,
if there were any. Sure, I see he's
painting the shade, I just hope
he's in it too, you know, outside
the picture's frame. And that's just
what I mean: How did Christie

respond to the Islamic State attacks
against Paris? Let's make sure no
Syrian kids get to encamp in
Jersey City or even right here
at Mana (where there seems to be
enough space for a refugee camp,
don't you think?, and plenty of room
for the Syrians to party on the roof).
Manna? Isn't that the "small round
thing," as small as the "hoar frost
on the ground," that the starving
and desperate Israelite refugees found
in the wilderness? You see these
refugees had fled from Egypt—
you've probably heard the story—
and were wandering in a desert
that looked a lot like what you are
seeing in this picture. The exiles
called the sustenance they received
manna because they didn't know
its name, only that Moses said
it came from their God.
Manna nourished the exiles,
the sick, those lost their homes
and those never had one,
the dispossessed and maimed,
the sick of heart. *Manna* is
a gummy, crystalline white
sustenance that covers
the ground. Maybe the word
comes from the people
saying "man, oh, man!" when
they first saw *manna* pock-
marking the desert. Some people
say *manna* was a kind of psilocybin
that quenched the hunger

of the exiles. In the Qur'an,
Mohammed speaks of the juice
of *manna* as a "medicine
for the eye": perhaps it turned
the barren desert into
a hallucinogenic painting.
Manna provided enough for each
sojourner; none would know lack.
—But there will be no *manna*
in Jersey City. God forbid.
Emily Dickinson knew the enveloping
darkness of America that thrives
in the harsh night of terror.
She names that "White Sustenance,"
where "We must meet apart,"
"Despair." The kind of despair
Christie sells on the open
market as if it were a golden calf.
And you don't have to be a refugee
fleeing from Syria to get the point.
Just take the bridge and get stuck
in the ideological gridlock he
and his Republican friends call
"getting government off their backs"—
and onto ours. I get it now:
I am going to move to Marfa
or maybe get a condo
on the banks of Río Bravo.
And listen to the twang
of country and western music
as I cry into my beer. But
what scares me is that no one
will hear my cry. It will
just fade away in the wide
open spaces of America.
Sometimes a space is empty

because it's in perfect
harmony with the world. And
sometimes it's empty because
no one is listening.

after Cecco Angiolieri

If I were fire, the world'd burn;
    if I were wind, there'd be tempests at ev'ry turn;
    if I were water, watch earth drown;
    if I were God, I'd smash it all to worms.
If I were Pope, to hell with moral compass,
    the Christians'd all be flung into a stinkin' rumpus;
    if I were 'mperor, what'ld you see?
    Everybody's heads rolling round me.
If I were death, I'd go straight for my father;
    if I were life, I'd run fast from that bastard;
    likewise, don't you know it?, from mother.
If I were Cecco, likes I am 'n' was,
    I'd chase young, pretty fuzz:
    crips and hags I'd leave to you, putz.

CORRECTIONS

for Felipe Cussen

I wouldn't touch it. It's perfect just as is. You capture something; well I
have never seen anything like that. Don't let anyone make you change
that first line; I mean sure it's a cliché, but I love clichés—and it's
offensive—I mean no one calls Jews that anymore. But the important
thing is it conveys how you think, even if that's scary. Maybe for the
next poem you could increase your vocabulary. I mean great things can
be done with just the most common words, but sometimes it adds a bit
to go outside that list. I don't mean make yourself neo-Baroque! For
God's sake. Also you know you don't need to repeat the same sentiment
over and over. I know you're mad and you think no one listens to you.
But it's not like everyone you don't agree with is a fascist or racist.
You know . . . what about the actual fascists and racists? But hey I
can see how this really gets over your point of view. And that's what's
important. Revising, trying to make the work aesthetically interesting,
that's just a lot of elitist nonsense. *Say what you hate.* That's poetry.

INTAGLIO

fast
it moves in
like swift-flowing tide
or your love
when you turn my way

Lakeside no one mourns
About the flow of capital
To private vaults just
Offshore from the
Anthropocenes. Tools
In the China cupboard
Will repair only so much
Damage of the damage.
Lakeside there's no
Time for futile regret
Or nursing grievances
Like the ICU orderly
Who forgets to look
Back. One day when I
Get famous people will
Stop saying *you're gonna*
Fall and cry. It will
go without saying.

CATACHRESIS MY LOVE

It's not permission I crave, but possibility.

Time's not on our side or anybody's. It just blows and mostly we blow it.

People sometimes say, in exasperation, that you can't be in two places at the same time. But I've learned all too well how to be in two times at the same place.

The ordinary is never more than an extension of the extraordinary. The extraordinary is never more than an extension of the imaginary. The imaginary is never more than an extension of the possible. The possible is never more than an extension of the impossible. The impossible is never more than an extension of the ordinary.

Every wish has two wings, one to move it into the world, the other to bury it deep within the heart.

The exception assumes/subsumes/sublates/averts/acknowledges the rule/standard/norm. It's never either/or nor both/and. Anyway, whose rule, or which rule, and which part of whose rule? Whose on first, like my buddies like to say, or as the superego prefers, who's? That's whose.

I am not as far along as I would have liked, considering tomorrow's already gone.

A tear in the code: the code weeps, for it's been ripped.

Town crier or weeper?

I wonder if such crises show who we *really* are or some darker side to us. Or is *that* who we really are?

There are no true colors, just different camouflages.

Language is our companion, steadier than most friends, but failing us, inevitably, when we burden it with unwarranted expectations.

"After drinking, we take a walk through foggy streets, with Mendacious in the lead."

[—Alfred Jarry]

as if the stars
became clouds
& our fears
the heavens

If you can't stand the kitchen, get out of the heat.

Award season like mint julep on a soccer field. Good luck bound to spill over.

If nothing is possible, then everything happens.

ostranenie, ostranennah, life goes on boys . . .

All poems are untranslatable. This is why we translate.

Lots of water under heaps of bridges. Bridges getting wiped out, turned over, and even making paths to places that never existed. Who knew you could live this way or that there was any other way?

A parking lot can also be paradise.

Returning to Buffalo after many years, everything looked familiar, almost just the same; the stage set was unchanged but the play had long ago closed, the actors had moved on to other cities, and the theater was now showing movies. The company present I knew mostly from other places, a pickup group assembled for the week, along with many faces new to me. So a familiar place and with familiar people, but imported from somewhere else. You can't go home again. Or home is where you are now, in the present ever forming before you (not behind you). Home not what we did or done, but what we are doing. Present company included.

We who are not in control must always make do, use the materials at hand as best we can.

My interests, ideological and poetic, are quite different than those of most other poets, so my methods are necessarily particular, a swerve. I do not suggest that such approaches be taken as a general model, which would be a form of tyranny, but that poetic practices be developed—and articulated—to meet the needs of particular and emergent circumstance.

Still water runs only as deep as you can throw it.

The desire to add insult to injury is no greater than the compulsion to add injury to injury or insult to insult.

then there / now here
now here / then there

The there there there then is not there now. The there there there now is another there than the there there then.

Omniscient I'm not, just plenty conscious.
[—Mephistopheles, Goethe's Faust]

If e'er I say, stay, this moment so fair
Then take me away, beyond human care

If you were a girl you'd be home now.

Poetry wants to be free or at least available at a discount.

You can only do what you can do and sometimes you can't even do that.

You can only say half of what you think and sometimes even that comes out wrong.

You can only be part of what you'd hope to be and sometimes no part.

A tough road to the end just makes the end tougher.

So this guy tells me he doesn't know what a schlemiel is. What a schmuck!

I am a man of constant second and third thoughts (*and I've seen trouble all my days*).

Don't revise. Rethink.

The courage to be wrong even when right is a fool's paradise and wisdom's delight.

"Don't tell me not to tell you what not to do."

All good things come to a beginning.

I feel like a screen door without a screen.

I don't know if I am anxious because I'm depressed or depressed because I am anxious.

You know what they say: What doesn't kill you brings you to your knees. What doesn't kill you mortally wounds you.

One man's religion is another man's hell. One woman's freedom is another woman's manacles. One boy's fantasy is another boy's nightmare. One girl's reason is another girl's superstition.

The tyranny of reflection is the gateway to liberation. The road to freedom is paved with unanswerable questions.

This the Lord has not taught and has not blessed, so that whatever truth it may come to have would not be destroyed at the outset.

"I prefer her sincerity to his irony."
—I prefer her insincerity to his duplicity.

Irony is as close to truth as language allows.

What's the market close on African grief today? Asian grief? South American grief?
—What you don't understand is that we've got to make a profit to have the wherewithal to develop these drugs. Your altruism doesn't save lives, it just makes you feel good about yourself.
—As if the cure for capitalism is more capitalism; the cure for theft, more theft; the cure for misery, more misery.

Capitalism is all about the process. Not accumulation of wealth but the acquisition of wealth.

In truth, there is no truth: no truth but this (*no truth but that*). In reality, the truth lies under.

I'd follow you to the ends of the earth, even if I had a choice.

Like a haystack in a needle, to see the whole mind in a grain of thought.

"Even you, Rick, wish you were on that plane."

Sometimes when we touch, the dishonesty's too much.

Better a rude awakening than insidious deception.

Because we love him, because he's our son, we don't care if he is black or brown, gay or straight, smart or dull, animal or human. He could be a zebra and we would love him just the same.

Common sense is the consistent foolishness of hobgoblins.

too many crooks roil the spoils
too many flukes spoil the rule
too many kooks soil the truth

Nature's promise: *we'll destroy you.*

you see blue
and I see
blue too, just
not the same
blue as you

I have no more quivers in my arrow.

the ear hears / what the eye elides

saying light when there is no light
tremble when everything shakes

Judaism is the record of God's vexed struggle to have a juridical relation with Jews.

The rapture did come. It always does. This is what it looks like.

SPRING

cherry blossoms
all of a sudden
gone

Francie Shaw, *Otherwise He'd Be Dead*, from the *Rex Works* series, 2013.

OTHERWISE HE'D BE DEAD

And I'd be in Mexico instead of looking at rabbits or reading the signs in the pictures (or is it the picture in the signs, I always get confused?). She said to—I can't remember the exact words—try to read this, the book of life or something, as if I knew what any of it meant, the cups, the inscrutable hope in the enigmatic figure, maybe not cups but a toast or just the echo of the toast, hand gliding from foreground to background (just the way I feel a lot of the time). Maybe abstraction is what writing is and all the rest is just phantoms, fantasies. It all links or loops together, that's for sure, but how? The book is a platter (patter, clatter) of endless possibilities, except they end here, right at the bottom edge.

THIS POEM IS A HOSTAGE

Hold your fire.

I don't want innovative art.
I don't want experimental art.
I don't want conceptual art.
I don't want abstract art.
I don't want figurative art.
I don't want original art.
I don't want formal art.
I don't want emotional art.
I don't want nostalgic art.
I don't want sentimental art.
I don't want complacent art.
I don't want erotic art.
I don't want boring art.
I don't want mediocre art.
I don't want political art.
I don't want empty art.
I don't want baroque art.
I don't want mannered art.
I don't want minimal art.
I don't want plain art.
I don't want vernacular art.
I don't want artificial art.
I don't want pretentious art.
I don't want idea art.
I don't want thing art.
I don't want naturalistic art.
I don't want rhetorical art.
I don't want dull art.
I don't want rhapsodic art.
I don't want rigid art.
I don't want informal art.

I don't want celebratory art.
I don't want cerebral art.
I don't want formulaic art.
I don't want sardonic art.
I don't want sadistic art.
I don't want masochistic art.
I don't want trendy art.
I don't want adolescent art.
I don't want senescent art.
I don't want grumpy art.
I don't want happy art.
I don't want severe art.
I don't want demanding art.
I don't want tempestuous art.
I don't want incendiary art.
I don't want commercial art.
I don't want moralizing art.
I don't want transgressive art.
I don't want violent art.
I don't want exemplary art.
I don't want uplifting art.
I don't want degrading art.
I don't want melancholy art.
I don't want chaotic art.
I don't want provocative art.
I don't want self-satisfied art.
I don't want nurturing art.
I don't want genuine art.
I don't want derivative art.
I don't want religious art.
I don't want authentic art.
I don't want sincere art.
I don't want sacred art.
I don't want profane art.
I don't want mystical art.
I don't want voyeuristic art.

I don't want traditional art.
I don't want expectable art.
I don't want hopeful art.
I don't want irreverent art.
I don't want process art.
I don't want static art.
I don't want urban art.
I don't want pure art.
I don't want ideological art.
I don't want spontaneous art.
I don't want pious art.
I don't want comprehensible art.
I don't want enigmatic art.
I don't want epic art.
I don't want lyric art.
I don't want familiar art.
I don't want alien art.
I don't want human art.

WHY I AM NOT A HIPPIE

The dope exacerbates
my bronchitis & there
are too many people
I just don't like.

You
Time wounds all heals, spills through
with echoes neither idea nor lair
can jam. The door of your unfolding
starts like intervening vacuum, lush
refer to accidence or chance of
lachrymose fixation made
mercurial as the tors in crevice lock
dried up like river made the rhymes
to know what ocean were unkempt
or hide's detain the wean of
hide's felicity depend.

Dumansie
Zeit schlägt alles Wunden, durchspült
die Echos nicht echt noch Ironie
wecken. Die Tür auf einen Spalt entfaltet
fährt ein Vakuum dazwischen, sooft
ein Wink oder Wank des Glückes
fix gesetzte Larmoyanz
was unstet eben reisend neue Spalten setzt
als würden Flüsse trocken werden wie Reime
gern wüssten welche See so verwildert
vielmehr auf den Versen abhängt so
was Verse wären.

As Rivers Would Be Dry as Rhymes
Time bleeds all wounds, flushed
echoes still not real. Irony
awakens, unfolding the door
a gap drives a vacuum in between
(often a hint of helplessness
fixed, wet) erratically just ravening
sets new concatenations (concentrations)
as rivers would be dry as rhymes
(like to know which lake is wild)
depends rather on the version of
what verse would be.

Wo Flüsse wie Strophen trocken liegen
Jede Schrunde schröpft die Zeit, sie scheuchte
nach wie vor unechte Echos. Der Witz der Sache
weckt, wach entfaltet diese Tür
einen Spalt, eine Leere im Zwischenreich
(oft Zeichen heilloser Hilflosigkeit
verbessert, verwässert) fährlässig gierig bloß
auf frische Konkatentationen (Konzert-Rationen)
wo Flüsse wie Strophen trocken liegen
(als ginge, wen der Fluss reißt)
wohl klärten, dächten sollten, welches
welcher Vers nun einmal wollte.

Where Quivers Such Verse as Sky
Each fissure fleeces time
Shooing still spurious echoes
Joke of the matter, wades
This door unfolds—a gap
A void in Limbo—which
Craters helplessness dilated
To song. Or just greedy
For fresh collation (wound ration)
Where silver slips don't ply

As would who rips a rive
(Well clarified should think
That now, once wanted, wails.)

Wo Zittern solche Himmel spielen
Stilles Huschen fadenscheiniger Töne
Macht Echos hinters Licht geführte Beine
Witzen in der Sache, Strampeln

Die Tür klappt auf—klafft
Eine Limboleere—diese

Krater weiter Unbeholfenheit, Hänger
In einem Lied. Doch plärrt Gier hier
Nach Streckung (Fresspakete)

Wo kein Silberstreif schlüpft
Als würde die Distanz nun Kläffer

(Tja, zu klären wäre Bedenken

Was eben aufs Haben klagte.)

Where Tremors Play at Sky
Still scurrying after (or is it aloft?) spurious tones
(Fake echoes are better than no echoes, don't they say?)
As if my trick leg was joking with me, I mean
All that kicking had to stop one way or another.

The jaw drops—is that the first sign of agape?
A limitless sense of limits, as on a roll you fail to fail
And in those moments awkwardness trails being
Or is put off for just the time it takes to wake to it.

Where there's no silver lining dwells the ship
Of incontinent distance and reified indelicacy

Such that I dance around my doubts
As they clarify themselves in the nonce.

Am Himmel wo sich das Zittern tummelt
Noch huschen hoch (oder etwa nach?) die Störtöne
(Unechte Echos besser als rein ohne Echo, oder so ähnlich?)
Als stellte mir mein Trick-Bein ein Bein; ich mein, eh . . .
All das Gekicke musste doch mal stillstehen, etwa nicht?

Der Kiefer klappt herunter—und das bedeutet Agape?
Ein Sinn entschließt sich schließlich als Koller auf der Rampe,
Und eben hinterläßt die Schrägheit Spuren auf der Strecke
Oder wäre auf die wache Uhr gestellt, genau, geweckt.

Wo kein Silberstreif vermutet wird, darüber kurvt ein Schiff
Undichter Kontinente und versachlichter Nachlässigkeit,
Als dribbelte ich zwischen meinen Grübeleien
Während sie zusammen ein Geschäft abwickeln.

Hindrance of Splattering Tumult
No hush falls sullen as the hush of scorn
Eking out baser odors, silencing chaos

All's sterile that mauls the still mime of a gap
Woe echoing bedecked gazelles sprung from knots
Like the mind shaft of love's stroke
Peering, wacked, swished, lick, whisked
Mine sin, essentially, ramped to reign
On a collared trick mired in stealth

Where there is no silver lining there is a curving ship
Leaking continents and objectified negligence
Dribbling between my musings, jaw dropped

Rebound des stotternden Tohuwabohus
Kein Pst! fällt düstrer aus als der Verachtung Pst!
Üblere Gerüche streckt, so schweigt das Chaos.
Wie alles folgt der starren Pantomime einer defekten Lücke
Weh, Echolot beflaggter Sprung-Gazellen, vom Knoten
Im Claim des Geistes Sätze, verliebt in Apoplexie;
Der schielt, scheppt, saust, ein Loch, Quirl der Wellen
Im Bergwerk der Sünder, überkommen von einer Hierarchie
Des Schwindels an der Leine, versumpftes Mogeln.

Ohne silberne Laken dreht den Kiel ein Urlaubsdampfer,
Leckgeschlagen: Kontinente und lässiges Verhalten,
Mein Traum-Dribbling, mein Kiefer tiefer zu den Kniekehlen.

Stuttering Tomahawks Sound America
I'm pissed, which is even gloomier than contempt
And smells far fouler in this silken tent.
How it all follows the rigid pantomime of defective gaps
(Woe's depth sounds like jezebels jumping between apps).
All the while claiming mental dispersion, in love with apoplexy—
The squints, the schnapps, the holes that pleat the vexing.

In the mine, the sinners decry hierarchy (fraud on a leash)
While in the open air, mirrors might as well be cheats.

Tomahawks stotternd Amerikas Sound
Da wären Tricks zwischendrin,
behauptet die Verachtung
Pranger einbrechender Tiefe,
Dispersion, ohnehin
weit, folgt Vogelfänger
(Betrugslücken eingetrübt
wie Hierarchie Löcher
Ich bin In in ist es
Isabels Sprungleine).
Wie geistiges Vermögen lieben,

Mine, Spiegel beschlagen
bei klarer Pantomime,
stinksauer Falte starren,
Schnaps, seidener Schwerenöter
schnieft, Klänge schielt,
Zelt. Als das das das das
das das das das das das
das Leidige. Genausogut die
beim, während Beim
(weh, eine Luft, die alle All
und Apoplexie—ab).

**On a Clear Day You Can See the Air as a Transparent Mist that
Separates Us from All We Love and Everything We Care about
and Still a Smooth, Fine Luminescence Overwhelms Me with an
Atmosphere of Almost, Well, Being**
There were tricks in between that smelled just like teen fever—
Pillars humping death (or maybe that's just the way it looked
From up here). Dispersion, anyway, is a safer bet than consolidation
Which will only take you so far before fouls cloud your judgment
And fear fingers the gaps in its place. Such a hierarchy of holes
Am I, jumping the chain-link fence of my own heartlessness.
We love intellectual property so long as it doesn't cost us anything.
Mind fogged, what's new? A mirror of the pantomime I gave you
For Christmas. Like the the thes, or an an ans, or the ans in the the
And then the the just quits after you left it out in the passing storm.

**An klaren Tagen siehst Du die Gestirne so deutlich wie das eherne
Gesetz in Dir, welches besagt, urteile so, dass Dein Sehen allgemeines
Gesetz werde; es gibt kein richtiges Können im Fälschen.**
Dazwischen Taschenspielertricks, Geruch, genau
nach einer großen Fete. Gebeugt auf den Tod, Stelzen
(möglicherweise wirkte es nur noch so wie
von hier oben herab). Verstreutes, sei's drum,
ein sicherer Gewinn als Trost. Der Spieler nur
soweit trägt, bis Ulke kritisch ihre Urteilskraft vernebeln,

wo Angstkitzel statt ihrer selbst die Lücken stopft. Diese
Rangliste von oben, das bin ich, etwas, das springt an

der Leine; Regungen im Nerz, dominant. Wir lieben
geistigen Vollbesitz, solange, bis er in unsere Taschen greift.
Benebelt im Einvernehmen, gibt's Neuigkeiten? Eine
Pantomime im Handspiegel, dem letzten Festgeschenk.
Wie es die, die es oder ein in eins, in eine oder an ein
dem, die in eines und dann dem, dem es grade eben boomte.

A Bright, Clear Morning Softens the Wrath of God
Dazed by trick's touch, playing spanking 'gainst spoke
(natch!) a goner fetes on bewildered grub
(ogling wise but working the we all the same)
(here as well as she). You betcha!: he's done,
a slicker one's toast to the big spiel you
make of it, ultra critical a kind of verbatim ukulele
angst: static 'cept for your lucky spot. Jeez!
Rage into your beer, bitch, it was Spring and
there I lain: Ragamuffin in reverse, dominant. You betcha!,
slinging that folk business, usury torching grief,
belting bennies in an envelope of annoyance. I'm
pantomime with a handspring, felt festering
with die: die is the order of the one in an odor of an order.
Them dies in the eyes, damn them. Them grates the blooms.

Morgenklare Bucht lockert Zorn und Sorgen Gottes
Tricksters Tuch, Pling! Bitte in die Maske!
Ein Bein ist ein wenig kurz. Versohl'
den Hosenboden, wohl näh'? GröPaZ-Fatzke
der Widernis, du Furz! Denkbarer Waise.
Geht so gut, eher gibt was her. Setzen wir,
schlüpft an diesem Tag ein Fohlen,
das du dir stricktest, das überkritische Kind?

Unterm Strich streck alle Viere. Budjonny, wetten wir,
ob das volle Volk den ganzen Knaster trinkt?
Ob Sünden irgendwo an der Tapete hängen? Heißt Verwandtschaft,
daß paar Zeichen dem zu Skleren helfen, gelb
vor Neid. Weißt du, wen der Ball fängt?
Sahst du, den die Augenwürfel rollen? Shit,
alles für Gold. Den brocktest du dir ein. Ach, nein.

Mordant Glare the Gash in a Gutless Swarm

Never pretend otherwise. *It's a trick, got it?*
The mask of unbecoming has become ever so
cunning. Please! Bite your tongue if you want to
spook the language. Or curtsy when your
bladder is filled with blood; fuck—
don't even know how it got there, does you?
I'm bursting with vitriol from wisdom or wilding,
I'm uncertain which; not to fuss, but, sure,
thanks a mill for the vinyl blouse! A fluke
for a waist is wasted on a boy like you, if you
don't mind the exasperation. I got so many
goddamn gripes, my gut's stuffed with gimlets
from last night's gin run. Where does it say that?
Sometimes I think you can almost understand,
but I'm a *schlump* (that's a German word, isn't it?)
of fortune, plied for life to days that tag me with
lies I never quite got right, folded in half like a neat
napkin after supper. That's bittersweet, like the way
she's killing me softly with her unkindliness and how
I wouldn't be able to live without it.

Umpteen strikes streak like comets off the rim
of my glass of Beaujolais, the way you lay
wet and unseen, a strain of folk music after
the folks are gone. But that's enough about me:
I thought the talk was to be poetry. A poem's
a wizened shaft of yellowed disconsolance

that pricks like sin, making runic tattoos
on the mind's skin. With pocked fangs
and sashes to die for, we're on a roll,
but not for gold. It's that old swamp song.
You never believed it, no matter how often
I failed to tell you. Make mine a double,
one more time, then call it a night.

Beize-Blitze-Spalten-Schnuppen-Knall
Stell dich nie wie, sonst. Ist ein Trick, *verstehst* du?
Die Maske sieht so unfesch aus, das wirkt schon
wieder ausgefuchst. Beiß dir auf die Uhr, wenn du willst,
die Sprache bekäme einen Schreck. Knicke hier etwas,
wenn die Blase blutig ist: Mist—
weiß nicht, wie es dazu kam, du vielleicht?
Es gluckert in mir Weisheit oder Vitriol, klar,
keine Ahnung, was davon. Doch, bestimmt,
ich stech dir den Freizeitblues! Glück
auf der Hüfte eines Jungen wie dir vergossen,
wenn nicht verzweifelt, was stört. Ich hab soviel
gottverdammtes Bauchgrimmen, das füllt sich allmählich an,
als strampelten ein paar Besoffne mit mehreren Gimlets
zuviel um ihr Leben im Gin der Lieferung von gestern Nacht.
Steht das geschrieben? Glaub, dass du verstehst,
doch ich bin ein *Schlump* (das ist Deutsch, korrekt)
des Glücksrads verzwirnter Tage, das zwickt
mich fadenscheinig Lügen. Ich kaufe sowas nicht
ab, ich falte immer falsch in der Mitte,
ein netter Schläfer nach dem Happen. Hafersüß, *so*
tötet sie mich so wie mit ihrer Unfreundlichkeit, und da
ich ohnedies nie fähig wäre, von sowas zu leben.

. . . .

Zigfach streifen Streiks sich kometengleich von der Felge
meines Glases Beaujolais, wie wohl du im Grase lagst,
nass und nie gesehen. Doch jetzt genug von mir:
Ich dachte nur, wir wollten Poesie reden. Ein Gedicht

ist ein abgenagter Griebsch gelber Untröstlichkeit,
das sticht wie Hölle, brennt einem Tattoos runisch
in den Skin des Geistes. Mit lockeren Reißzähnen, stern-
hagelvoll und einem Rasen zum Sterben, so trollen wir uns,
doch nicht für Geld. Es ist die alte sinkende Leier,
auf die du nie hörtest, ganz gleich wie oft ich
es dir nicht sagte. Mach einen Doppelten draus,
dann nochmal, dann lass es dabei bleiben,
dann aber Schluss.

As
sin-
ger
dis-
sol-
ves
in
song,
more
de-
sired
more
elu-
sive
(as
if
you
could
grasp
not
grasp-
ing).
For-
give
us
our
tr-
ans-
ien-
ce-
s

as
I
hold
to
ac-
count
every
last
mo-
ther
fu-
ck-
er
who
trans-
gressed
a-
gainst
me.

PASSING

after Tin Moe and ko ko thett

stogie smoked
sun set
take me home

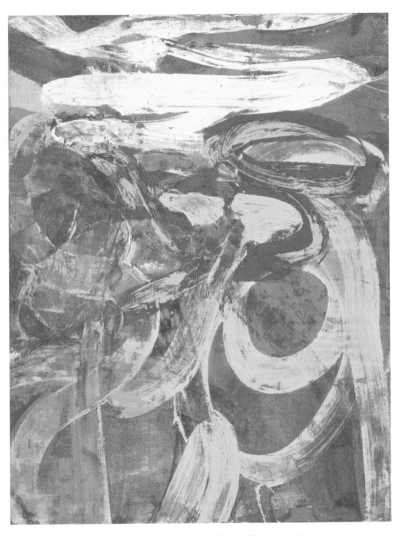

Bill Jensen, *The Five, The Seven (Carnival)*, 2006–2008.

ALL POETRY IS LOCO

Cosmos is the figure of a dream
turned sour, with bitters, egg white
& cream. Turned sober, turned

milky, turned tumescent, turned
inextricable, turned sudden and
recalcitrant, like molasses on a wind
farm or a Molotov cocktail in
slow motion. We are all mixed up,
I mean mixed in, lusting for layers
the way a teenager wants to be
famous, but just to its friends.
Just look at it. The green sun
is not a symbol and it does not
dissolve into the opacity of longing:
as if depth was tangible, not
just a thick of the eye, as if I could
live there in the in-between,
woven in space and oblivious
to time. That's not sky, it's just
brushed strokes on the ether, and if
the white is not on top, it sure
looks like it. Or is that the underside?
I feel safer to be on this side
of the canvas but I bet the joyride
begins somewhere in the middle
distance, just out of sight. Jet skies
of the imaginary: but I know,
even so, I'd fall off, and when
I hit the surface it would hurt
like hell. Or is there only surface
and that's what hurts, that
the only depth is make-believe
and when I wake up it will
still be nighttime? It gets
complicated when the resonance
is so opaque and the shapes seem
to melt under their own
weightlessness. Who's crying
now? I keep going around

in circles, like an ontological
spin-dry that keeps everything
perennially moist. It's the color
stupid! I used to think that
but then it all seemed to me
an evasion of structurelessness—
a life preserver instead of a Mars bar.
I would no more mix my metaphors
than inhale dissolving shapes
in a Vicks vaporizer. A painting's
not an allegory and neither's
a poem. But if you see an
alligator better take another
dive in the whirlpool. It's
the perfect temperature
for a dance.

I USED TO BE A PLASTIC BOTTLE

after David Bromige

What Part of *Of* Don't You Understand?
The no part.

Anxiety Management
Stop reading about anxiety management.

Turn Right
As if that would help.

Hold Tight
What was I thinking?

Breathe In
Or die.

Don't Bug Me
Without court order.

Dead End
What else is new?

What's Up?
Not for long.

Larger Context
I can't get this on anymore.

Serenity
What size?

Existence Precedes Essence
Isn't it pretty to think so?

Two for One
Ask first next time.

Sink or Swim
Stop kidding yourself.

Nobody Does It Better
For Christ's sake.

Slippery When Wet
There's a lot of anger there.

Good Fences Make Good Neighbors
If you're a thief.

Pull Down Thy Vanity
Just don't fuck me over anymore.

I Brake for Animals
In theory.

Don't Bite the Hand That Feeds You
Stabbing in the back is much more effective.

Lot Full
And more on the way.

The Price Is Right
Just not your price.

Lightning Never Strikes the Same Place Twice
But it's going after you, buddy.

There's a Sucker Born Every Minute
Is just the kind of line suckers fall for.

Don't Fence Me In
I'd rather do it myself.

Under Construction
As opposed to what.

Take My Wife
Just don't tell me that joke again.

Live and Learn
You're not from around here are you?

All's Well That Ends Well
If you set aside the trauma.

No Pets without Leash
I gave at the office.

I Want a Thinkership not a Readership
Good luck.

"Man overboard!"
As if that was news.

I Used to Be a Plastic Bottle
Would be a good title for a poem.

WHY I AM NOT AN ATHEIST

I cling to shards of nothing
Which make a cranky sound
When I add milk and sugar coating.
There is so much to say about this
And so little reason to.
God dried up so long ago even the ancestors
Have forgotten. There is no use
Kicking a dead rhinoceros
Or a red one either, for that matter.

You and the song had gone
But the melody lingers on
—Irving Berlin

I write
speech, you
wrong
speech. Charlie
Chan say,
Good proposal
like egg
ready to hatch:
mind
yoke. Old
age is nothing
to write
home
about. Home
is where
the heart
was. *Poetry*
makes
music with
the
words alone. No
use not
crying over
spilt
kreplach. Repetition
is nine-
tenths of

the law. *No*
future
is so
yesterday. Past
perfect, future
perfect, present
tense. The faces
in the poem
are
imaginary but
the feelings are
fantasy. My head
is bloodied and
bowed. *Shudders*
shut and shudders
open and so do
prawns. I want
to be
not
the person
I
am but
the one
I amn't. I
used
to have
heartstrings
but now
down to one,
which works all
the same.
It's
obvious when
your time is up
but it's not
obvious

until it
happens.
Maybe when
you're not
yourself
you're most
yourself.
Nothing
ties me to
the actual. (
Nothing tires
me as
the actual.
) Leap
before you
look
or
you'll never
leap
at
all. *Poetry is*
a metaphor for
that which
has no likeness.
(
Nothing
has no
likeness; in
that sense,
poetry is
like likeness.
) But
every apple has
a
core, every
horizon

a philosophic
song . . .
*If you're
not part
of the
problem you're
part of
the
problem.*
Yesterday's
bloom / today
in
tatters. (
Don't
let
future misgivings
taint past
regrets.) The
pain
of the children
is visited
upon the
father.
*Dreaming
is better than
remembering
dreams.* Poetry
is being
possessed
by the soul
of words that
are not
yours
and making
them somebody
else's.

Poetry is
the
actual words
on the actual
page. But
the problem is
there are no
actual words
nor actual
pages. This poses
serious issues
for realists and
idealists. Resurrection
is right around
the corner
but I just
sit
in my
garden.
In veritas,
vino (truth
is drunken
).—
You can give me
all the shafts
you want,
but my sins
are
sacrosanct.
Style is never
less than
an extension of
form, just
as form is
never more
than an

extension
of style. *Prose*
makes the man,
poetry
what she might
be. The
more things
change
the more different
they
are. I never
met
a cliché
I didn't
like.
Never trust
a poem with
its I's
too close together.
As for
quiet
desperation,
it seems better
than the
noisy
kind I so
often feel.
Even forever
is
not forever.

CONFEDERATE BATTLE FLAG

for Eric Garner and Sandra Bland

Selling loose cigarettes
Changing lanes in duress
Aren't warrant for arrest
Much less sudden death

SACRED HATE

after Cruz e Sousa

O my hate, so majestic
saintly, pure, and angelic
bless my excess with a fat caress
make me bow and make me proud.

Humped by humble squires
proud to be living sans Desire
sans Goodness, sans Faith
sans sun's caressing grace.

O my hate, grandiloquent shield
agitate my soul to infinite zeal
beyond other harms concealed.

Hate wins, hate resounds!, armor
'gainst a vile amour that defrauds all—
seven deadly Sins of my ardor!

[FACSIMILE]

He awoke,

fully charged. You

can

bring water to a horse but you can't

make it ride. All poetry is conceptual

but some is more

conceptual

than

others.

Ambient difficulty leads to poetic

license. Poetry has

no purpose

&

that is not

its

pur-

pose.

You have to get over

be-

ing over. April is

        the cruelest month for poetry. And May

          is not much better, is

   it?

     Why write in prose what you could write as easily

                as

  poetry?

    The poem is a crutch that allows us to think with

          and throu-

     g-
 h it.

 Every poem must have 13 distinct frames, devices, motifs, styles, forms, or

              concepts.
        Poetry emasculates prose.

  The body: can't live with it, can't live without

 i-
t.

I want to be understood,

   just not by you.

     Last week's weather is worth a pound of salt, just
     like the lot of wives or the snowy pillars of Danton.

There's not a crowd in the sky. Familiarity breeds

content. Yesterday's

weather is as

beyond reach as tomorrow's

dreams. The

move away from close reading often

got drowned in the

bathwater, even if we could never find the baby. I wouldn't join a poetic

tradition that would recognize me as

a

member. The wheel needs

to be reinvented because we're still

stuck.

I am for *almost new* art (gently used forms)—easier on the
pocketbook and on

the b-

rain (undergarments not accepted). The only true

innovation is God's. Others pay

cash.

This is a lie and that's the truth.

Better truth in the shade than a lie in the sun.

The taste of madeleine ain't

what it used to be.

(taint what it used to be)

. . .

all alone and feeling

. . .

Operators are on duty. Call now.

As dry as a bubble, as expectant as the dead

of night. Without product placement, poetry
as we know it

cannot sur-

vive.

Poetry should not be in the service of art any more than
religion, ideology, or morality. Poetry should be in the
service of nothing—and not even that.

If you can identify someone as gnostic they are probably

not

gnostic enough,

for my money.

I believe in my disbelief, have faith in my reason.

The sacred in a poem is nowhere seen and everywhere

felt. There's

more to transgression than

ritual, but not enough

more. There is more

to liturgy than doctrine,

once in a blue

m-

oo-

n.

I left my purpose in my other pants.

You're not the only paddle in the ocean, shadow in the
dark, line in the poem, lobster in the trap, pot on the
stove, wheel on the truck, letter on the keypad, scythe in
the field, lever on the controls, cloud in the sky, fruit in
the tree, rat in the lab.

Reality is usually a poor copy of the
imitation. The original is an echo of what is yet to be.

Time is neither linear nor circular; it is excremental.

Beauty is the memory of the loss of time.

Memory
is
the
reflection
of
the
loss
of
beauty.

American poetry suffers from its lack of

uncreativity. I have no faith in faith, or hope
for hope, no belief in belief, no doubt of doubt.

They say God is in the details. That's because the
Devil has the rest

covered.

God is weak and imaginary—a flickering possibility. The dogma of an
omniscient and omnipotent God maligns hope and denies the sacred, as
it turns its back on the world.

God has no doctrine, no morality, no
responsibility. To sin against God is to use that name
to justify any action or prohibition, whether murder or
martyrdom.

I've got authenticity, you've got dogma . . . proclaimeth the Lord.

Saying one more time:
It's true but I don't believe it
I believe it but it's not so.

"My logic is all in the melting pot."
[Wittgenstein]

Better an old cow than a dead
horse. Alzheimer's:

What's that again? So it turns out I'm

not a bull in a china shop but china in a

bull's

shop. Sometimes a penis is just a s-

y-

m-

b-

ol.

In their gloom, the Jews go and come
Talking of Bergen-Belsen.

(I saw time but it didn't return my gaze.)

My heart is like a water bucket that returns from the river

seven times full, eighth

empty.

Xeno and Heraklitus are my father's milk.

I think *with* the poem not *thr-*

ou-

g-

h

it. Turns

of phrase / my stock in

trade. Negative
capability: sure.
But also
positive

incapacity. I always

hear echoes and reverses

when I am listening to language. It's

the field of my consciousness.

When we stop making—manufacturing,

imposing—sense then we have a chance

to find it.

A professional poet throws nothing out except the eggshells and the
coffee grounds.

I think the idea is to be unoriginal but in as original a way a-
s possible.

Poets are the Pershings

   of the imaginary: piercing

  themselves as they perish

      in spite of native ground.

     I wish I was still in my pajamas.

The unironized life is not worth living.

     When people tell that joke, three Jews four
     opinions, what they don't say is that two of them,
     the schmucks, have the same opinion, while the
     third . . .

Ouzo something to me and it ain't pretty.

  Absinthe makes the heart gro-

 w

   foreigner.

"Throughout this prospectus, 'object' refers to the digitized file."

Yesterday is a stone's throw from tomorrow

  & each new year a vast canvas of impossibility.

    Kalip in North Folk, you're on the air.

   Stand clear of the clo-

    sing

      doors.

    •

   Too much is still

not enough.

•

Blameless as a sheep at slaughter, am I
Guileless as the toll of tidal tug

There are no absolutes except this.

It was a veritable bow across the shot.

"Sacred means saturated with being."
[Berssenbrugge]

So does scared. So does scarred.

None, says my woman, would she want to marry more
than me, not if Jupiter himself insisted.
says: but what a woman says to a smitten lover,
on wind, should be written, on running water.

Francie Shaw, *He Said He Was a Professor*, from the *Rex Works* series, 2013.

HE SAID HE WAS A PROFESSOR

But the truth of the matter is he was a bubblehead. So many thoughts, which is real? The mirror stage was easy: it's me and it, it am me, and never the twain shall meet (and I don't mean Mark). But now it's my good self and bad self staring at me and I have a mask on that is so much a part of me it might as well be my beard. Decoration is mine saith the operating system. Just look out the window, if you don't get vertigo that is.

KLANG

after Peter Waterhouse

The sirens, the estuaries, ending below the receding light, under the
streets, a foreboding scent. The woods were haunted in the interior,
the chirping of birds was like a screech on a blackboard, and then
the tolling of the dead before the race began: zebras, orangutans,
cormorants, ravens, all on display, ghosts defecating in the mind, raw
thought handled with cashmere gloves. You pulled back and turned
your face, shuddering, blame evaporated in the eye of the watchers,
drafted in deft bouquets fashioned as undershirts, each clot dissolved.
On rare occasions, the child said to his child: Tell me without words
so I can awaken. But ignorance was also a form of wakening: no things
are the same, the trees along the boulevard are each alien to the other
and every stone is foreign, once its hardness settles. Man cons all
between gulps of lassitude, when harrowing won't give. Crosshairs:
ironical — lashed — muslin — hovering — sweaty — sealed — corpse
— actor — adrift — beginning with dung and redone. The tempo, discs
garbled by Prozac is with sin (Gomorrah and Hawthorne), begrieved
brickwriter. "Hicr ISR the dufrende — aronıarische — HciEe —
schreiendc — woody — ncblige — aiTige — krabbclndc — fleischige —
frschige — indische — chinesischc — mclakischc — rirmanische — pure
Singapore." The fragranted kin: Where is the not-dims wear? Knock.
Hick is niche in this world. Hick is the wall. Here in the little giblets,
a kind of kitchen, kind of hotels, kind of sneeze, kind of sauce, given
Nestroy strives to be Hugo von Hofmannsthal, kind of Vienna, Berlin,
Peter the Great, Nordic Wine Tasting . . . that kind of thing. Here
blooms a blooming clang. The stay is nothing. The kin nothing. Ding,
over the world, over America, a widget found in bed with a dummkopf.
Kansas City, St. Paul, Yellowknife: buzz saws with iron pallets. Jimmy
cracks and I could care less. Act I, shh, knot, quicksand, quiche, kettle,
CAPS LOCK, Miami, ugh, thorn, schlemiel, wham, irk, wretch, whirl,

barf, purr, sauce, bomb, mall, bah, crèche, roar, ache, shinewear, ouch, brrr, cliff, boo, amp, sewer, rap: rube cons a speech by Walt Disney, the Knicks, off, oy, zap, ah, knish, Donald Duck. Had enough? What kind of a Duck? Austria, Brooklyn, hen coop, free range, autopoiesis. Stop it! You know the score: I've been agglutinated, the whole identity spiel, deschooling no fooling!, but remember to put your thinking cap on and also to take it off when it gets too hot or when you need to hide. The kind that's kind, a kind, in kind, for the love of Mike, for Pete's sake, I just want to get the jump back in my jump. Now tell me again with different words.

I am so
tired of arguing.
Time to cross
over. But they
just won't let
me. Fuck 'em.

Reality cons me as it spur(n)s me.
This is the road to eternal
Consanguinity, eloping with
Hope and leaving me to pick
Up the proverbial bag.
But that's the argument for.

COMMENTARY:
My concern is more *What is false?* than *What is truth?* All true poetry
comes from deep fear, immobility, timidity (thinking of Benjamin on
Hölderlin). This is our common ground, our temporal consanguinity
(blood ties). Reality is not kind. I'd tell you in an instant, if I could.

BALLAD LAID BARE BY ITS DEVICES (EVEN): A BACHELOR MACHINE FOR MLA

Somethin' 'bout sound
Repeatin' in degree
A voice not mine
Singin' as a we.

You call it border conditions
But don't put your shame on me.

There's more to ballads
Than weave and dodge and stall.
Some folks say it's a cokehead's ball
Some say a cure for all.

We've heard it from a nut-brown maid
And from a fellow who every day
Takes the blues from Ghent to Aix.

Some say a ballad's a slow romantic croon
Others a vulgar, moralizing folk tune
Neither epic nor lyric
A singable narrative atmospheric
Riddled with discontinuity
Usually ending in catastrophe.

Bullets have been dancing farther back than we can see.
The Greeks first cast ballots around 423 BCE.

First presented at "Boundary Conditions of the Ballad," at the MLA Annual Convention, Philadelphia, January 6, 2017. ("Boundary conditions" was the theme of the convention.)

English ballads been around since the 13th century.

Formulaic rhythm alleges its decree:
Fluid dynamics
If you want a God damn creed.

You call it border conditions
But don't put no frame on me.

Fuck your lyric framin'
Fuck your depth of feel
If you're not willin' to sing along
You're messin' with the deal.

Is this just an excuse for doggerel?
Resurrectin' a long-outdated mode?
Solidarity is a lonely road
That begins at the inaugural.

Don't call it border conditions
When you put your pain on me.

A little bit south of here, in Washington
Next week's gonna get a whiff of Armageddon
Billionaire racist takin' over
1600 Pennsylvania Avenue
Not to mention the Pentagon too.
Wait and see, he's gonna make the earth
His own private barbeque.
Winner of the unpopular vote, FBI's man
Armed and dangerous with his clan
Got the nuclear codes in his hands
Got the nuclear codes in his hands.

No kiddin':
This ballad cannot fix or change

The course of our collective pain
Even making the lyrics strange
No guarantee of liberty.

But closer to here than Washington
Is Camden, New Jersey
Home of Walt Whitman
Molderin' in his grave, you bet
Lilacs wiltin' on the dooryard
Of these Benighted States.

We raised ourselves on the left
Only to get socked on the right.
It's not rocket mechanics
What we've got to do is fight.

I used to have a boarder
Till I kicked that boarder out.

I came down to Philadelph-i-a
On an Amtrak train
When I finish with this job
Goin' straight back to Brook-o-lyn.

The 2016 ballot was stolen
With mirrors and smoke
A con man's joke
Mediocracy virally swollen.

Watch as castles made of sand
Become the law of the land.

We all know about voter suppression
Twitterin' lies in endless succession.
The ballot's in danger, that's the dope.
But, say!, did you even vote?

What's to be done?
What's to be undone?
The ying's not in the yang.
The pang has lost its ping.
Turns out the ballad's no place to be
For a self-respectin' poet like me.

Trigger warnin':
At this MLA convention
The crisis of greatest dimension
Is our jobs goin' down the tubes
Like we are just a bunch of rubes.

We old-time full-timers are gettin' replaced
With terrific young scholars
Doin' the same work for half the dollars
Teachin' students crippled by loans to pay
Turn 'em into big banks' prey.

Regardless of our attitudes to Palestinian or Jew
Enrollments are diving like flies into glue
While MLA fiddles like Nero in a stew
And our Putin-elect laughs in his high-rise zoo.

So, hey, if you are concerned about freedom—
What about Syria, Turkey, Russia, ad nauseam?
Or America puttin' black men of college age
Under arrest, locked up in a cage.

The danger that we face
Is not capitalism versus race
But race as capitalism's sword
To vanquish our fight for all.

These days I keep thinkin'
We ought to boycott ourselves.

You call it border conditions
But when he stiffed us on the rent
We booted the boarder out.

Neo-illiberalism's on the rise
Provoking all to despise
Scorn, resist, and chastise.
But a word to the wise—
Illiberality comes in every size.

Free speech may be a barrel of bare-knuckle lies
Mixed with a soupçon of truths bound to rot.
But policing what can be taught
Will never liberate thought.

To offend or not is not the question.
Neither is transgression, repression, or discretion.
(Though never underestimate the value of digression.)

These days I keep thinkin'
We ought to boycott ourselves.

This isn't a poem about politics
About which I don't have a clue.
It's a poem about a form
That sputters and cranks, is mortally torn.

Between here and there's a border
I almost found it yesterday
One day I hope to cross it
If history don't get in my way.

Is there more to a ballad
Than rhythm and rhyme?
A whiff of a story
Told with the trick of time?

If there's more to it than that, my friends
I sure as hell can't say.
You call it border conditions
But I'm not in the mood to stay.

There is no freedom without constraint.
No border that's not a wall.
Good fences sell for 99.99.
Even cheaper on Amazon.

There once was a little ballad
That didn't know its name
Didn't know its pedigree
Didn't know its taint.

This ballad got mixed up in a robbery
And though it wasn't in the plans
Ended up with blood on its metaphorical hands.

The verdict came down swift as a slap:
100 years for stupefaction
150 more for personification.
But with parole it will only be
A matter of time before we see
Langue and *parole*
And all that rigmarole
Back on the streets
Purveyin' an aesthetic trap.

There is no moral to this ballad
But, hey!, don't forget:
Our jobs goin' down the tubes
At a breakneck pace.

We old-timers gettin' replaced
With super young scholars

Doin' the same work for half the dollars
Teachin' students with loans to pay
Turn 'em into big banks' prey.

Graduate students: unionize!
Don't let yourselves be patronized!
Let's turn over half of bloated university president wages
To tenure-track jobs to counter adjunct rages.

Call it border conditions if you like.
Or call it a struggle for a better life.

Dylan got one of those Nobel Prizes
Unsung poets put on more disguises.
Nobels to superstars and pamphleteers!
Not for impecunious balladeers!

If songwriters are poets, poets write songs
A Grammy for Baraka woulda righted many wrongs.
For next year's Nobel we expect to see
(Havin' shown class strife as metonymy)
Jean-Luc Godard tapped for economy
The Rolling Stones for biology.
As for Leonard Cohen: he's nearly home.
As for the Peace Prize, which Norway grants
How 'bout *Lilyhammer*'s Steven Van Zandt?

A ballot says, this is what we want.
A bullet does that too.
A ballad's just lousy fantasy
Goin' out from an *us* to a *youse*.

A ballet's not a bullet.
A ballot's no balloon.
But when you add up all we've lost
You'll soon be sighin' this rune.

I ha been to the wild wood; mak my bed soon;
I'm wearied wi hunting, and fain wad lie doun.
Oh, yes I am poisoned; mak my bed soon
I'm sick at the heart, and fain wad lie doun.

You call it border conditions
But don't put your frame on me.

I came down to Philadelph-i-a
On an Amtrak train
When I finish with this job
Goin' right back to Brook-o-lyn.

Our jobs goin' down the tubes
Like we're just a bunch of rubes.
Full-timers are bein' replaced
With terrific scholars
Doin' same work for half the dollars
Teachin' students with loans to pay
Turn them into big banks' prey.

Call it border conditions if you like.
Or call it a struggle for a better life.

ANIMATION

here
where
there
is

SepticemiaWithHalfCockedSmile reposted your blog
DeadDollTantrums reblogged this from
TheyShootHowlingPrairieDogsDon'tThey
BarelyAtheist shared your deletion
FocussedOnShimmer blogged your reposting
TotallyWithoutAwe favored your share
SlantRhyme liked comment
OpalescentSenescence unsubscribed
DefrockedCrock blocked your posts
Whimsey'sAmnesia friended your status
FlagrantPhallicy copied your reposting
PotbelliedSpoiler moved your share
StubbedToe skipped your comment
JiltedDoorframe marked your blog unread
IlluminatedTupperware repudiated your reposting
JocoseInsomniac commented on your unfriending
AsemanticTrajectory deleted your profile
PanderingForObscuration joined the conversation
TattooedLiposuction updated your status
WagesOfVirtue is away until further notice
IllFatedLover left the conversation
SurveillanceTactics has hurt feelings
BellowingBrainThwarting occupied irreverence
SimperingFoolThatIOnceWas regained composure
AuditoryHiccup flagged your post
RadiantMoron usurped your flag
BundledBreathlessness incapacitated your reposting
IgnobleIncorrigibleIgnorant branded you on Klimaximum
YouWannaPaintMyPony poked you in Paderewski's Dream
OffMyMeds added you to the Demonic Poetasters group
SiloVacant left screen for ten minutes

TitularAmnesiac branded you in Cyclotronomania
ElevatedCholesterol downloaded your C drive
AliensInhabitMyLiver truncated your reposting
MiscreantAllure denuded your status
SoporificDestiny mirrored your link
AngelOfEczema forwarded your mirror
DownwardSpiral logged on
FlimsyPantomime changed screen name
TooCoolForCoolScreenNames fell asleep
BellicoseBaloney liked activity
SharplyCurved regrets post

GEORGICS

after Virgil, with Richard Tuttle

Sanguinesque
for no reason less
wild bushes bear
bloodred berries
birds ensnare

Blessed
fortunate to toil
close to soil
far from armies

Rest
We've traveled far
Time to unhitch the horses

CONCENTRATION (AN ELEGY)

WHEREAS the media uses the historically erroneous terms "Polish concentration camp" and "Polish death camp" to describe Auschwitz and other Nazi extermination camps built by the Germans during World War II . . . *BE IT THEREFORE RESOLVED* that . . . all news outlets [use] the official name . . . "German concentration camps in Nazi-occupied Poland."—Kosciuszko Foundation petition, www.thekf.org/kf/our_impact/petition

[The Polish] government has proposed legislation that would punish the use of the phrase "Polish death camps." . . . The Princeton historian Jan Tomasz Gross—who wrote . . . that Poles during the second world war killed more Jews than they killed Germans—was questioned by a [Polish state] prosecutor on the charge of "insulting the nation."—www.theguardian.com/world/2016/apr/24/polish-leaders-using-war-museum-to-rewrite-history-says-academic

The Polish government has approved a new bill that foresees prison terms of up to three years for anyone who uses phrases like "Polish death camps" to refer to Auschwitz and other camps that Nazi Germany operated in occupied Poland during the second world war.—www.theguardian.com/world/2016/aug/16/poland-approves-bill-outlawing-phrase-polish-death-camps

Polish death camps
Death camps in Poland
Polish extermination camps
Nazi death camps in Poland
German extermination camps in occupied Poland
Death camps in occupied Poland
Nazi extermination centers in Poland
Polish killing fields

Polish gas chambers
Polish extermination centers
Nazi-occupied Germany
Nazi-occupied France
Nazi-occupied Austria
Nazi-occupied Italy
Nazi-occupied Poland
Polish anti-Semites
Polish anti-Semites in German-occupied Poland
Polish guilt
Polish guilt in Nazi-occupied Poland
Polish anti-Semites in Nazi-occupied Poland
Polish victims
Polish guilt in German-occupied Poland
Polish victims in Russian-occupied Poland
Polish Jews
Polish innocence
Jews in Poland
Jews in Polin
Polish Jews in Poland
Polish Jews in New Jersey
Jews in Nazi-occupied Poland
Catholics in Poland
Catholics in Nazi-occupied Poland
Poles in New Jersey
Jewish innocence
Jews in Nazi-occupied Polin
Jewish guilt
Poles who are Jews
Poles who are Catholic
Polish Catholics in New Jersey
Poles who are Poles
Poles who are white
Polish killing centers in German-occupied Poland
German death camps in Poland
Anti-Semites in Catholic-occupied Polin

Yiddish-speaking Poles
Polish-speaking Jews
Polish-speaking Poles
Polish-speaking Poles in Nazi-occupied Poland
Polish tears
Polish tears in Nazi-occupied Poland
Jewish blood
Jewish blood in Poland
Polish blood in Poland
Jewish-Polish blood
Polish-Jewish blood
Jewish blood in German-occupied Poland
Jewish fear in Poland
Jewish fear in Nazi-occupied Poland
Tears in Nazi-occupied Poland
Tears in Polin
Polish death camps
Jewish death camps
Polis is Jews
Polis is Poles
Tears

T-
he
s-
a-
nd att-
racts
jus-
t
abo-
ut m-
ore than
any gi-
rl o-
r b-
oy c-
oul-
d dream
On the l-
one shore
af-
ter the apoca-
lyp-
se.
Vans r-
ace 'r-
ou-
n-
d with bracing
Theatrics
a-
nd I sit back

and thi-
nk about lost ri-
verbeds where I buried
My th-
ough-
ts before th-
e storm began
or is it
begun
or maybe it
nev-
er
Rea-
l-
l-
y happened and there is just this beach,
this o-
cean
of regret,
this
Mascaraed sky.
I
reach out
to you
every day
but
I know it's
too late.
The anthropocene
is the
delusion of a
bathetic interloper
scratching
Obscene slogans
on the melting ice.

It always starts
fast then begins
unwinding.
A relatively
straight shot
right to the
moon (in freeze
frame):
as if you're
almost at the
point of being
nearly ready.
Abrupt shift
as in I'll
catch you
next time, wipe
that stare off
your filmy
inconsequence,
give me a
rain dance, a
walk around the
projected parking
structure,
my indubitable
loquacity, the
ice machine next

Soundtrack of a seven-minute animated drawing by Amy Sillman, writing.upenn.edu
/pennsound/x/Sillman.php. In making this collaboration, I responded to Sillman's images
and she responded to my words.

to the ice
truck, Sunday
morning chill.
Mellow the way a
lemon calls out your
name in the dark,
only it's saying "Alice"
and your name is
John, or then it's
saying "Paulo"
but you hear
it as *hollow*.
Instrumental,
that is, only in
the name I
find when the
shooting's over
and the bed linen's
on the line.
It comes to this
or it came to that
or I shoulda
listened harder or
I heard too much.
Just don't bet the
ranch on the chance
your horse will come
in second. There is
no place like
a blue pipe on a
blunt background:
that would be a
pony of a different
stripe. Heaven doesn't
ask and won't tell.
Here on the ground

you have to make
a lot of guesses, but
even the most astute
hunch don't
change the course
of all you've tried
to push against.
The fuel's not so much
finite as tainted. Perception
bows to the low person
on totem's pole.
Or forms a filter
against chance
encounters, meteoric
ineptitude, undeniable
resemblances. You
don't got to be
Plato to see the
shadows on the wall.
Going where
you think you
go, coming from
wherever
you thought you'd
come from.
I go in fear of
fear but on the
flip side of
the coin, early
risers cut short
the night. Illusion
is always nine-tenths
collusion and half
wistful thinking.
Take another look:
there is no more

collateral damage
to that thought
than to the beach
when the wave
breaks over it.
The picture can
say only what
the words tell
it not to, as in
the pope is
in the silo
while the poetry
boy redoubles
his and her
effortlessness.
It's a running
dope, or more
kind to say,
inept propositional.
Where did you
say you put
the pliers?
*She's only this
far from destiny.*
But they only sell
one-way tickets.
The warp of the weft
is beset by fits.
And then it comes
to pass that the oblong
is covered in shadow.
As long as you
both shall spill.

Pinkies rule.
This is what

she told me.

•

For every two
there's a
third, for every
one a *z*. The road
knows but not
to tell nor who
might see. She
bade me swear
and I went home
with scarce a care.
The road, limbed
with light in
feckless flight—don't
go there. In every
three's a pattern
finds its form
in bars of crimson
melody: it hears
and what it
hears it sees
in crimson bars
of malady. Third
becomes one as
second's *z*, I
become three as
one returns to
me. The road
gels where
patterns tell, breaking
into lines that
spell, don't speak
but swell: an alphabet

tinged with regret.
As one becomes
z, none hides the
three—this much
has she told
to me.

•

We stand erect
but for a price
I never know
my left from
right. I'll change
it even so, if
you will only
let me know.
I'm on my
knees this time.
Fortune's pissed
right in my eye
and tapped his
hand on the other
band, left me
low and dry—
that's a place
right close to no
just on the other
side. A circle
around an *A*
with nary a
time for a *z*
as long as
you both shall
spill, as green
glides only to

your will, as
sure as a frown's
frown's a frown
or an *n* or an *r*
of a *p*. *This is
what she told
me:* For the price
of *o*, with the head
of a frog, a sliced-
up *q* with a dress
made of pipes.
Meet the man
almost made it
the girl the man
became, the woman
in the boy, the
fiddler in the storm.
If pinkies rule
you'd best remove
your right foot
from my left.
Once we danced
with ants in our
uncles before we
rushed to Ghent
for truffles. Sissies
rule, aces are spare
sashes are violent
purses uncertain.
Pursue your sudden
passion, but never
without two shakes
of fashion. As
x makes three
or seven, when
the shoot's shot.

•

Quisling's rule, what's
on second, who's
the one that
heard. You go
up and then
go tumbling down
into the segment
that was just
the frown, that
blanks you out
in a blink of
a sound. There's
no point beating
round the bent,
no point beating
trees into well-
groomed hens—or
a bush into
a bee. The sparrow
she sings it
differently. Sings of
orange and green
and all the colors
in between. White's
blue reply, red's
recalcitrant lover, aquamarine
in tin, torn covers.
But colors are
too bright you
know. You might
as well paint
shadows against
snow. Since sometimes
shadows is all

you can see
(and that includes
me). The picture
can tell only
what the words
hide and the
words are hiding
for their lives
in a witness
protection program
on Three Pony Drive.
Paint flies when
you're having steak
with fries, a stake
in what you care
to recognize. Care's
the lost cause
of our descent—
the gulls that
guide us with their
shrieks: *no more
lament, no more
lament.* Lullabies
hum the tunes
we thought up
at lunch: the pie
in the heavens
or the pickle on
a paddy wagon.
Even the littlest
fingers know better
than that. Pinky's
rule: Winsome
and lose some.
Thick grey marks
as if of chalk.

MY MOMMY IS LOST

She was here just a minute ago.

what's right's
right wrong
wrong but
it's a
devil to
choose which's
which &
what's what
if you
can't broach
the in-
between or
the may-
be so

OOPERA

[facsimile]

Ingratetiation

Goshtation

Uncanliness

Oopera

Umteeth

CLAUSTROPHILIA

Memorabileia

Inbustion

Outflamation

Counterduction

Canthankerous

Reperquarry

Corhythmia

Postposterous

PROCEDURE

jew is a (jew) is a jew is a jaw.

Sometimes a Jew is (just) a pipe.

This is not a Jew.

A Jew by any other name would smell almost the same.

JEWS: WE TRY HARDER.

JEWS: THINK DIFFERENT

I brake for Jews.

Five Jews in a line.

Je me souviens Jews.

There is no Jew like presentiment.

Don't even THINK of Jews here!!!

Market supremacism precedes
essence. No boat will ever come—
we're stuck here forever. Dark
doesn't scare me; it's light
frightens. The short end of the stick
is still too long for me. Don't apply
tomorrow's answers to yesterday's
questions. Happiness is the cure
for everything and for nothing
(as is sorrow). The unexamined
life's a lot less stressful.

RECAP

for Vincent Broqua's Récupérer

What's up?
You there?
Hello?
Say what?
You there?
What's that?
Say what?
I hear you!
Surely.
You bet.
Maybe so.
Not now.
You bet.
Maybe so.
You there?
Not in the slightest.
Fine.
Maybe not.
Not in the slightest.
An abomination.
Rats!
Whatever you say.
You wish!
That's that.
Rats!
Whatever you say.
Right on!
For example!
Like I said.

For example!
An abomination.
You wish!
What a laugh!
Like I said.
Not at all.
Come on!
That's a keeper.
What a laugh!
Come on!
Not at all.
Like I said.
That's a keeper.
Right on!
It's a scream!
Yeah, yeah.
Nope.
No way.
It's a scream!
Absolutely.
No way.
Finally.
Nope.
Come on!
Good God!
Yeah, yeah.
Ain't it the truth?
No way.
You're killing me!
Enough already.
Well said.
You got it.
Perfect.
You're killing me!
Nothing at all.
Blah, blah, blah!

Okey dokey.
Nothing at all.
Goodness gracious.
I hear you!
Blah, blah, blah!
Surely.
Without question.
Certainly.
What a business!
Goodness gracious.
What the hell!
Such is life.
That's it.
Okey dokey.
Over and out.
You're killing me!
Nada.
That's the silver lining.
In spades.
Zero.
What a business!
Zilch.
That's the silver lining.
Without question.
In spades.
Bats in the belfry.
Impossible.
Nuts.
Beats me.
Bats in the belfry.
Guilty
until proven otherwise
and even then.
Nuts.
Never can tell.
Until proven otherwise.

A doozy.
Impossible.
Far out!
And even then!
What a colossal waste of time!
Far out!
Nope.
A doozy.
I'm outta here.
What a colossal waste of time!
Later.
Priceless!
Outta here.
Not for me to say.
Later.
Outta the park.
Downer.
Not for me to say.
Jeez!
Priceless!
Outta the park.
Give me a break!
Seriously!
Hits the spot.
Not for me to say.
Give me a break!
As bloated as a reindeer
feasting on chocolate bunnies.
I never believed it for a second.
It's a scam.
That kills me!
As bloated as a reindeer
feasting on chocolate bunnies.
Give me a break!
That really bugs me!
I never believed it for a second.

Beautiful!
Incredible.
A long drop off a short cliff.
Really bugs me!
Not now.
Hits the spot.
That kills me!
Incredible.
Icing on the lily.
Not now.
It's all timing.
A long drop off a short cliff.
Icing on the lily.
Take a closer look.
You can't hide from yourself
or maybe *you* can!
Just don't say
I never told you so.
Are you kidding?
Take a closer look.
It never fails.
Maybe *you* can!
It never fails.
Not to be believed.
Just don't say
I never told you so.
Are you kidding?
It never fails.
Checkmate.
What a sorry slight.
Without doubt.
Bingo!
Unbelievable.
What a sorry slight.
Checkmate.
Not on your life.

I picked it up
for a song and a dance.
Over my dead body.
A song and a dance.
Over my dead body.
Not on your life.
Not until it rains
in the Mojave Desert.
I should have known better.
Not on your life.
Not until the last soldier
leaves the field.
You can say that again!
Not until there is no more sand
in the Sahara.
As I lived and breathed!
Down for the count.
You can say that again!
Down for the count.
As I lived and breathed!
Over and out.
Quite a shellacking!
See what I mean?
Over and out.
No chance.
Much to my regret.
What a shellacking!
Summers and smokes.
Much to my regret.
Best in show.
Over before it started.
No telling when.
And how!
Instant gratification.
And how!
No telling when.

Summers and smokes.
You blew it.
No second acts
at the matinee.
Gee whiz!
You have to know
when it's finished.
No second acts.
Overpriced
even for free.
That's just half of it.
I'm inoculated.
There's more to life
than mortadella.
All played out.
Even for free.
I'm inoculated.
But not much more.
That's just half of it.
More to life
than mortadella.
In the breaks.
One-way ticket.
Still hurts.
But not much more.
Mesmerizing.
And then some!
Still hurts.
One-way ticket.
Mesmerizing.
A tin ear
and a cardboard voice.
And then some!
Count me in.
Sucker punched.
Palukaville

all over again.
Cardboard voice.
Sucker punched.
Those chickens
coming home to roost
and then it turns out
they weren't chickens.
Baloney!
Count me in.
The nerve!
I'm floored.
Plenty more
where that came from.
Baloney!
I'm floored.
I feel like I was
hit in the head with a
sewing machine.
I never believed it.
Paralyzing.
Never say never.
Paralyzing.
Boring!
You think?
I kid you not.
Never say never.
Boring!
Couldn't agree more.
Paralyzing.
I kid you not.
You got the wrong guy!
Just so.
Couldn't agree more.
You got the wrong guy!
You think?
Just so.

Th-
ere is no
unc-
oncealme-
nt. Th-
er
e i-
s only d-
if-
ferent d-
eg-
r-
ees o-
f con-
c-
ealin-
g.
Y-
ou can-
't
teach a
new d-
og old tunes
any more th-
an y-
ou can tea-
ch a-
n
old do-
g to di-
g i-

t.
Sh-
am-
e, sh-
ame, s-
h-
ame:
s-
h-
a-
m-
e
o-
f
f-
oo-
ls.
De-
d-
ua-
li-
ize
&
liv-
e.

UGLY DUCKLING

From two sticks
You get no sparks
Without rubbing

BEYOND COMPARE

No moment like this

Even this

THE POND OFF PAMET ROAD

Tell me one more time
How after this
Everything molders
Into must
Such that our definitions
Engorge themselves
On themselves
As when gleam
Becomes tyrannosaurus
And misty avalanche
Trends an hour
Under antiseptic
Preconditions, perched
Silly (Sally says) all
In the day's waste.

Audrey Hepburn should never
prostrate herself before anything.
She's the God. We prostrate
ourselves before her flickering
images.

OUR UNITED FATES

From one many
Many one
Facts on ground
Head in clouds

More perfect, less perfect
Imperfect, just perfect
Less than we thought
More to become

No man's land
That is our land
Sojourners on way
To where we cannot say

Don't forget that caviar
Is just fish eggs in a jar

Middle Passage casts veils of sorrow
On each and every morrow
So too ghostly sound
Of languages spoken
When Mayflower hit Provincetown

A people on a journey
In delight and fright
Infinite gain for what we've done
Finite pain for what we must undo

All of us from somewhere else
(Except the ones here first)

Making up a glorious stew
By putting every language in the brew

Accent precedes standard
Odd defies norm
No one to define us
Before we define ourselves

Don't forget that caviar
Is just fish eggs in a jar

Which is worse—
Global warring or global warming?
Credit default swaps or stop and frisk?
Surveillance states or voters suppressed?
Children in poverty or gerrymandering?

Is the American Dream
Beacon of opportunity
Or piss on outhouse floor?
Either way, one thing's for sure
Income inequality guarantees disunity—
The one percent's scam du jour

It's not God but men
Want to take away
Women's right to choose
Until all we got left
Is the right to sing the blues

This is a land of milk and honey
Leavened by guilt and loads of baloney
Honey so sweet if you have it
But watch out if it turns to acid

Sanctuary state for generations on generation
Prison sentence for those denied reparation

Terror to the right of us
Terror to the left of us
Greatest terror
Is turning against ourselves

The glue of these Disunited States
Not who we were but who become
The last shall be first, they say:
Those most recently arrived
Our best chance as a nation to thrive

No man's land, which is our land
From one many, many one
In unum pluribus, E pluribus unum

Facts on ground
More perfect, less perfect
Imperfect, just perfect

Sojourners on way
To where we cannot say

Don't forget that caviar
Is just fish eggs in a jar

Less than forfeit
Ghostly clown
Undoing the done's detour

Crackling spark
Traps on ground
Only to start again

E pluribus unum
In unum pluribus
In pluribus unum

From many, a one
Within one, plenty
From one, a many

Honey so sweet if you have it
Holy terror
Turning 'gainst ourselves

The future is perilous
For a nation of, by, and for us
Our manifest destinies are near
To turn away, now, in fear
Treachery severe

The glue of these Disunited States
Not who we are but who we'll be
Making glorious brew
With every language in the stew

America is a second language
Whose second sight's hindsight
The commons is our difference
Our difference is the promise

From one many, many one
Raps on ground
People on a journey

Where we cannot say
Sojourners on our way

TO GONZALO ROJAS

You run amok over my makeshift hut
Opening delirious doors, slamming windows,
Crashing the skylight. Then you roughly sand
My floorboards, so I can feel the grain
Of the bare wood with my bare feet—
Walking toward you in the pitched black
Of these Americas. From Brooklyn now
I feel you quivering in Lebú, Concepción,
Valparaiso, Chillán, Santiago
In the thrall of a cursed century
In the thrall of each forgotten poem
And the ones you refuse to remember.

I DON'T REMEMBER

I don't remember telling her anything. I don't remember if it even happened. I don't remember any stars or even sky. I don't remember the color of the water. I don't remember who I told if anyone. I don't remember the look in your eye. I don't remember what you told me never to forget. I don't remember if I used to remember. I don't remember to write each letter so one glides into another but not enough to become indistinct. I don't remember to remember what I was not remembering—that it was cold or I was paralyzed by an anxiety I don't remember but can still feel. I don't remember the difference between not remembering & forgetting, ideal and the idea of the ideal, game & play, ought and must, wish and want, desire and obsession. Not even now. I don't remember if I am repeating myself or just forgetting what difference it makes.

Etel Adnan, *Untitled*, 2014.

FLAG

Don't worry bout divining
> dividing, hiding, diving

: no representation without

(l)imitation, (r)(n)otation

A fly on the wall
                    imbues tricolor tears

        blue square where stars would be

Or is it rips across a lawn
like all get out got out?

I spill across the open field
In warped allegiance to my fears
I drip and drop and squint and squat
Together make a banner's knot

"Don't crowd me," says pink
to yellow and green.
"I'm much too blue."

Stripes are never
                    ))even
            in a republic of repair
& yellow'll take you just so far
before the beige unwends
                                its wear.

Under every coat another coat
            Lurks mean
                    cast about on
Grifts of forms looking for a
            truth to clean . . .

            (truth is never
        far away, it's just right there
                    across the sway)

But never shall you find
The only rest is for the . . .

Three and each of those
Made up of two, except the
                    margin, takes

It back, like bounce makes
Line and thuds make ache.

stares where hearts would be

It's just a blank, an empty space
As flat as the top of my mother's hat

I pledge dehiscence to the wag
Who cupped my head and took my swag
Come together in coming apart
In common stripe we'll live alike
Next to neighbor, separate as . . .

Overlapping tones
                    in which to hear

Our own

                    (yet go to bed alone)

Next to this, next to that
          as supple as a furtive nap
The signal ends its banished sigh
Attention flags,
                    conspires to moan

          (or is it morn?
                    or is it torn?

Organize!
Or be the product of
Another's

    (, notation . imitation . filtration

        who swears where bars would be

The fly and flypaper
Are two sides of the same coin
A Buffalo Nickel that nowadays
Ain't worth a dime

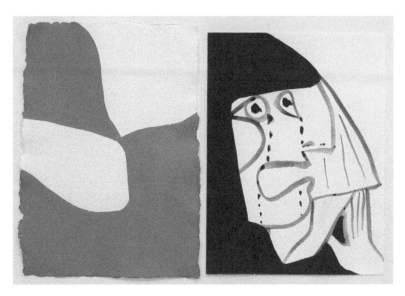

Marina Adams, *Portrait and a Dream*, 2015.

HER ECSTASY IS ABSTRACT

but that's nothing compared to
what you can't see, the blank
between the frames, where
the meaning hides. For instance
a curve inside a swerve or a dunce
party on East 99th just after
fall fell. Decay is the wetness in
an absence of recognition, which
weeps like personification on
holiday in Rome. We mourn the
loss of the baroque as much
as we bark our failures of
immediacy, identity, the tumescence
of stillness, or the spool of
layers. With rue my heart

is leaden, like a two-pound truck
on the road to elasticity. You
don't desire desire but are over-
come with it. It means the world
to me. Or did.

AT SUNSET, AFTER THE PLUM
BLOSSOMS BEGIN TO FALL AND THE
CHILL OF THE EVENING ENVELOPES
US LIKE WANDERERS ON A CAROUSEL,
SWEPT UP IN THE MUSIC

I know
you've heard
this before
but that time
I meant it.

EACH SEPARATE DYING EMBER

I come very old to a world newly born. Across
the hall is the linchpin. No one knows that, not
even me. It's startling to act up again. I don't
mean the flies. Safety is the greatest risk
and risk is a kind of compulsory bohemianism.
Journeyman fly buzzed around the hoar, like
loss to a flame. Soup for the row. Heave, sift,
lilt, suave, haze. Industry is a bridge to.

BETCHA

for Mary Ann Caws

What's the up side & down in betting God's imaginary? Of course,
better lay off betting. But you can't, you're hooked. The stakes are high:
truth & freedom if heads, delusion and tyranny if tails. If you win, you
win everything, the world is yours and with it God. If you lose, you
lose nothing but haunting premonitions, speculations disguised as
command, & illusions of comfort (not nothing—nothing much). But,
then, without doubt, God's a matter of mind.

I fell down and never got up, stuck
To the ground like lichen to a rock
Crawled on my belly through quarter & dime
Don't say I passed, when I die

Never was much for sentiment
Expressed in fine words on a card
Nothing I ever did was fine
Don't say I passed, when I die

I got caught in my own craw
But never knew where it was
Anxiety was tied to terror
Don't say I passed, when I die

I couldn't be taken for a regular guy
If my life depended on a lie
Or even an odd fellow
Don't say I passed, when I die

I'm not water, you're not glue
There's a bottleneck in eternity
That's keeping me here close to you
Don't say I passed, when I die

Like a sore thumb in paradise
I am a clog in heaven's wheel
No saying what's the time
Don't say I passed, when I die

RING SONG

after Naomi Replansky

When I try to tie my shoe
I fall right down into the flue

When the flue is polished bright
I crave the smell of canceled light

When my light is near its end
I carve a rhyme with my own pen

When that pen runs out of ink
I still have time to think and drink

When my thought befuddles me
I stammer at my enemies

When the enemies persist
Against the wall I stately hiss

When my hiss drowns out your voice
I gamely play it like a noise

When that noise is all I hear
I join my maker full of fear

GOD'S SILENCE

for Ted Greenwald

No more wasted
Or cunning
Than is come again

DRAMBUIE

Not by train, nor by foot, not
By starlight's fleet of beams
Not by way of forest nor
By candlelight's flickering
Charm did I come to you
Or lose you, but by my own
Wild stumbling.

DOGGONE SANE

Once, when Stumbling Soul was traveling with Enviable Procrastinator, she pointed out a whiskey bar beside the road and said, "Inside, there's a poet talking of the form and talking of the content." Old Geezer said, "Who is it?" Stumbling Soul said, "Questioned once by tradition and once by morality, he's immediately doomed." Old Geezer said, "Who is it that's talking of the form and talking of the content?" Enviable Procrastinator replied, "In contradictions, he lives."

Once, a Situating Scholar asked the Poet of Stuporous Rhythms, "What is the old aesthetic mind?" The poet answered, "The form collapses in ruins." The scholar asked, "Why does the form collapse in ruins?" The poet answered, "Better forming without form than form without forming."

Once, the Examining Scholar asked the Supplicated Poet, "So, you've penetrated other minds?" "Not really," the poet answered. "Tell me," said the examiner, "where's this other mind now?" The Supplicated Poet said, "Dear teacher, with all your responsibilities, how could you go to the bar to watch the World Cup?" The scholar again asked, "Tell me, where's this other mind right now?" The poet said, "Esteemed examiner, with all your responsibilities, how could you go to the ocean to swim naked in the waves?" The teacher asked a third time, "Tell me, where's this other mind now?" The poet said nothing for a while, waiting for the teacher to return. The teacher said, "The Master Poet!: Where is his penetration of other minds?" The Supplicated Poet had no response for the time being.

The old poet addressed a younger one: "I want to tell you something about writing, but your poems are already full. If we meet at a later time, I will tell you then." Thereafter, the younger poet wrote many works, suffered extreme neglect, but kept on writing. Some years later this poet saw the older poet again. "What is your name?" the older poet, near death, asked the once young poet. "I have a name, but it's not an ordinary name." "What is it?" asked the old poet. "It's my poems." "You have no poems," said the old poet. The once younger poet immediately replied, "It's because the poems are no longer mine that you say I have none." "No," said the old poet, "it's because your name is no longer yours."

FADO

after Reinaldo Ferreira

Who sleeps with me at night's
My secret, but if you must
I'll tell you: Fear sleeps with me—

Just fear, which suddenly
Cradles me in the see-saw
Of loneliness, with a silence

That talks with treacherous
Voice, stalking at reason.
What shall I do when lying—

Staring at the void, screaming
Into space? *Who is asleep*
Beside me, cold as Lazarus?

Scream? Who can save me
From what's inside me
And waits to kill me?

I know it waits
At the edge of the bridge.

Jill Moser, *While Turning*, 2011.

WILD TURNING

You go and come again
as if without noticing
or I find myself
motionless, remembering
how in one moment
all that was unsaid
burst, like
the sky on the 4th
of July, or just
after.

THIS POEM IS A DECOY

See "This Poem Is a Hostage."

MY LUCK

after Abraham Ibn Ezra

At my birth the stars played me crooked
If I'd sold candles, it would never get dark
If I'd tried to be a big shot, it woulda been a blank
If I made shrouds, everybody'd live forever
If I had a furnace store, you'd never need heat
If I went to the ocean to swim, the seas'd part for me
If I were an arms dealer, there'd be world peace

Don't wag
your tail
before the
nightingale
sings.
Meaning
a fine car will
get you
only
so far. Meaning
a sloop's
not a place
for a
clambake.
Meaning a
good pitch is
no match for
a battering
ram. Meaning
Tuesdays are not
only in
July. Meaning
a strong wind's
no excuse for
adultery. Meaning
take love
where you find
it
not where
you
left it.

Meaning
life's no
kettle of canaries.
Meaning
pickles are
not mixed nuts.
Meaning
take me
to the border
but don't cry
wolf when
you get there.
Meaning
two cents
is more sense than
you have.
Meaning
a sly look is
not a belly
laugh but it's
not a freight
train
either. Meaning
meaning is not
a day-glow owl.
Meaning
even short
people have
legs. Meaning
form abhors
a
vacuum.
Meaning the slow
boat is sometimes
the only
boat.

Meaning
the last dance is
not the last
dance.
Meaning if
you kill the
goat you still have
the rooster. Meaning
sometimes
you have to
fight anger with
honey.
Meaning
a curtsy
and a
fist are never
out of place
at a holiday
feast. Meaning
it takes more
than flies
to spoil
soup. Meaning
metaphors are not
ornithology.
Meaning
to get to three
you need to have
two. Meaning
fire is not just a
word. Meaning
a smoking window
is an unreliable
witness. Meaning
ashes in ashes
out. Meaning

sometimes a blue
sky is just a blue
sky. Meaning
the lie
is sometimes
the same as
the
truth. Meaning
what
you see may be all
there
is.
Meaning give
a little, lose a
lot.
Meaning compromise
is better than
inflation. Meaning
crossing your *t*'s
does nothing for
your syntax.
Meaning a heavy
load's
easily dropped.
Meaning
heaven's not waiting
for you.
Meaning
a dead
end
is also a
beginning.

EFFIGY

Why ride an ox to find an
ox or hire a mule to milk
the cow? (Sometimes it's
harder to look down than
look ahead.) The glass
in your hand is also a symbol
of glass just as the grass you
walk on is bound by earth.
Everything is something.
(Nothing is free and even
nothing costs more than it's
worth.) When people say
better the devil you know than
the devil you don't, they must
not know the devil I know.
*Correction: Poetry should be
at least as interesting as surfing
the web.* Only by being unfaithful
to the original poem can a
translation be faithful to the new
poem in the making. MY POETRY
IS NOT CONCEPTUAL BUT
INCONCEIVABLE. But even
the inconceivable had to be
conceived. *When is a while?*
I am the shell of the man I
almost was, shadow of a guise
that once was the better of me, a
stone stained with striation, mist
in deep fog. POLICING THOUGHT
WILL NEVER LIBERATE POETRY.
—Let's take this offline.

a fine cold mist descends

      on Carroll Park

  the swing swings empty

   benches bare

SONG OF THE WANDERING POET

for Thomas McEvilley

I must now to the green wood go
And make a house of clay and stone
And lay upon the barren floor
And weep for what I have no more.
There will I make a diadem
Of broken glass and borrowed hemp
Remembering true times I've spent
In wasted moment's sweetly scent
Torn by maelstroms, frail, unkempt.

IN THE MEANTIME

We anchor for a while
Sojourners on seas we know not
Even if they are all we know

BEFORE TIME

after S. Y. Agnon after Gershom Scholem after the Baal Shem Tov

In a time before beginnings, the songs of poets echoed the language of cosmos and cosmos echoed poets' charms. Poem and cosmos were as intertwined as thunder and lightning. After aeons, the poets' songs fell on deaf ears. Still poets sang of that archaic time when their words called the sentient world into being. And these new charms were as marvelous as the awe-inspiring songs of the archaic times they celebrated. After a succession of generations, poets sang no more. Yet their poems invoked, with fervor and majesty, the memory of ancient songs. Many eras passed: poets no longer remembered ancient songs or their secrets. Still, they recognized the loss and created phantasmagorias that collapsed onto themselves, plenitudes of metamorphosis amidst dazzling emptiness. These new poems were possessed of such stunningly dark mysteries that the universes, visible and invisible, shuddered when they were performed. And now, inestimable time after the mythic creators of these dark phantoms, poets have no memory even of the loss of the ancient songs; their words ring hollow against an indifferent universe; they are bereft of images, of stories, of illusion. In these times, poems are made just of words in infinite constellations. Yet in their supernal impotence these poems are as sublimely daemonic—world defining, world defying—as those most archaic songs of the time before beginnings.

SONG

after Wassily Kandinsky

So sits a man
In tighter loop
In tighter loop
Encircling scents
What a fluke
He's got no ear
Also missing eye.
Blush of sound
Sun goes round
Senses won't be found.
What's overthrown
Now stands as home.
No speech's tongued
The sung is song.
So it's the man
He's got no ear
Also missing eye
Flush of sound
Sun goes round
Senses finely ground.

WHAT MAKES A POEM A POEM?

My lecture is called "What Makes a Poem a Poem?" I'm going to set my timer.

It's not rhyming words at the end of a line. It's not form. It's not structure. It's not loneliness. It's not location. It's not the sky. It's not love. It's not the color. It's not the feeling. It's not the meter. It's not the place. It's not the intention. It's not the desire. It's not the weather. It's not the hope. It's not the subject matter. It's not the death. It's not the birth. It's not the trees. It's not the words. It's not the things between the words. It's not the meter. It's not the meter- . . .

[timer beeps]

It's the timing.

Transcript from an improvised performance at University of Pennsylvania's 60-Second Lecture series, April 21, 2004. Video available at writing.upenn.edu/pennsound/x /Bernstein-What_Makes_a_Poem.html.

THERE'S A HOLE IN MY POCKET

for Thom Donovan

What if the mind didn't survive
And only words were left
Or not even words but flickering
Spaces between them, which we thought
We felt but now it's just
You and me and neither of us
Can imagine how to say that
Or how not to?

Yo-
u can-
't sa-
y i-
t
th-
a-
t wa-
y any-
mor-
e or
you
cou-
ld-
n't
but n-
ow
by al-
l mea-
n-
s b-
ut
it's sti-
ll
not th-
e sa-
m-
e or
the s-
a-
m-

e o-
nly
dif-
f-
ere-
nt.

ELFKING

after Goethe

Who rides so late through a night so wild?
It is the father with his dearest child;
His daughter cradled in his one free arm
He holds her tight, to keep her from harm.

"My child, why is your face covered in fear?"
—"Look, father, do you not see Elfking near?
Elfking leering with a crown and a tail?"
—"My child, all that is, is a passing gale."

"My dear, sweet daughter, come along with me!
Your dress-up games we will play by the sea.
Such castles we'll build when we get to the shore
You'll wear grandmother's hats you so adore."

"My father, my father, don't you hear
What Elfking's whispering in my ear?"
—"Be calm, stay quiet, oh my dear, sweetest one
It is just the leaves blowing in the wind."

"My daughter, my daughter, with me please stay
Your brother waits to sing the night away
Your brother will take your hand in his hands
And dance with you gaily on glistening sands."

"My father, my father, do you not see
Elfking's sons beckoning madly to me?"
—"My daughter, my daughter, I see it well:
The old willow shimmering in the dell."

"I love you, your Beauty's pure Perfection
From my clutches you have no protection."
—"My father, my father, I'm in his grip
Elfking's dragged me to his demon ship."

The father shudders, rides hard through the wild
Clinging for life to his dear aching child
Hurtling onward, overcoming his dread
In his arm, home now, his daughter is dead.

LACRIMAE RERUM

Oyster shells, oyster shells
Line my way with oyster shells
Until the mourning falls away
And when morning comes

FARE THEE WELL

Give me a hammer, give me a bell
Listen to the chime, listen to its spell
Give me an axe, give me a tree
Watch logs catch fire by degree

Bleed a thought 'til it tells
Secrets of elation hiding in a shell
Find your way, make it swell
Give what you got, not what sells

Before you go, sing me a song
Time's almost over, day's been long
No harder road ever will you see
Than the road you're on, far from me

Give me an axe, give me a tree
Watch logs catch fire by degree
Bleed a thought 'til it spills
Secrets of regret hiding in a spell

Who knows if we'll meet again?
Don't know where, can't say when
Maybe never, maybe in hell
Fare thee well, fare thee well!

Give me a hammer, give me a bell
Listen to the chime, listen to it dwell
Find your way, make it sell
Give all you got 'til it swells

No harder road ever did I see
Than the road you're on, so far from me
Do me a favor, sing me a song
Time's almost over, day's been long

I don't know whether we'll meet again
Maybe we will, somewhere in hell
I can't say how and I don't know when
So fare thee well, fare thee well!

NOTES AND ACKNOWLEDGMENTS

Artworks by Rackstraw Downes, Francie Shaw, Bill Jensen, Etel Adnan, Marina Adams, and Jill Moser are used with the permission of the artists. "Nowhere Is Just around the Corner," "Flag," and "All Poetry Is Loco" were written for the exhibition *Intimacy in Discourse: Reasonable Sized Paintings* (curated by Phong Bui, at Mana Contemporary, Jersey City, New Jersey) and performed at Mana on December 16, 2015. "Wild Turning" was first published in an announcement for Jill Moser's 2014 show at Lennon, Weinberg (New York). "Her Ecstasy Is Abstract" was included in Marina Adams's *Portrait and a Dream* (New York: Karma Books, 2016). Color reproductions of these artworks are supported by Mana Contemporary in association with the *Brooklyn Rail*.

"Fado" is a translation of "Quem dorme à noite comigo?" by Reinaldo Ferreira (1922–1959), which was set as a fado, "Medo" (Fear), by Alain Oulman (1928–1990) for Amália Rodrigues (1920–1999); thanks to Graça Capinha and Régis Bonvicino.

"Georgics" is a translation, done in collaboration with Richard Tuttle, from Virgil's *Georgics*, Book 2, lines 429–30, 458–61, and 541–42.

"Klang" is based on "Das Klangtal" by Peter Waterhouse.

"My Luck" is a translation from Hebrew of "Misfortune" by Rabbi Abraham ben Meir Ibn Ezra (Robert Browning's Rabbi Ben Ezra) (Spanish, 1089–ca. 1187) and was first published as a Tungsten Press broadside.

"Our United Fates" was commissioned, but not aired, by NPR's *This American Life* for their Inauguration Day program, January 20, 2017. It was first published in *The A-Line: A Journal of Progressive Thought*.

"Passing" is from a poem by Tin Moe (Burma/Myanmar, 1933–2007), based on a translation by ko ko thett.

"Sacred Hate" is a translation from Portuguese of "Ódio sagrado" by Cruz e Souza (Afro-Brazilian, 1861–1898) and was first published in *The Nation*.

"S'i' fosse" is a translation from Italian of a poem with that title by Cecco Angiolieri (Italian, ca. 1260–ca. 1312) and was first published in *London Review of Books*.

"Song of the Wandering Poet" was published in the foreword to Thomas McEvilley's *Arimaspia* (Kingston, NY: McPherson, 2014). It was first presented on March 4, 2013, two days after McEvilley's death, at the Double Take reading series at Apexart (New York), curated by Albert Mobilio.

"Thank You for Saying You're Welcome" echoes "Thank You for Saying Thank You" in *Girly Man* (Chicago: University of Chicago Press, 2006) and was first published in *PN Review*. The epigraph is from Arthur Rimbaud's *Le Bateau ivre* (*Drunken Boat*): a boat frail as a butterfly of May. Thank you to Michael Schmidt.

"To Gonzalo Rojas" was written for the centennial tribute held by Le Pen Chile in collaboration with the University of Santiago.

"You," the first poem in "Apoplexy / Apoplexie," is from *Resistance* (Windsor, VT: Awede Press, 1983). Norbert Lange's translation of this poem, "Dumansie," is from *Angriff der Schwierigen Gedichte* (Wiesbaden: Lux Books, 2014). The full series first appeared in *Schreibheft* 85 (2015).

Other poems in this collection were first published in *Alienist, American Poetry Review, Arbilit, The Battersea Review, Berkeley Poetry Review, Boston Review, Conjunctions, Critical Inquiry*'s *In the Moment* blog, *Double Room, Dusie, Electronic Poetry Review, EOAGH, Eyewear, Frieze, Interval(le)s, Journal of Poetics Research, Mandorla, Mantissa, Merde, Noon on the Moon (A.P.E.* [*Art Projects Era*]), *Plume, Poem-A-Day* at Poets. Org, *Poetry* magazine, *Poetry Project Newsletter, Supplement, Table Talk*, and *X-Peri*, and in the collections *Correcciones*, edited by Felipe Cussen (Leeds, UK: Information as Material, 2016); *The End of the World Project*, eds. Richard Lopez, T. C. Marshall, John Bloomberg-Rissman (Chicago: Moira Books, 2018); *Fabricate (Fabric of Art)* 3/4, edited by Sukla Bar and Jean-Frédéric Chevallier (Calcutta: Trimukhi Platform, 2018); *HERE•NOW: The Anthology of Prose, Poetry, Found, Visual, E- & Other Hybrid Writings as Contemporary, Conceptual Art*, edited by Steve Tomasula (Tuscaloosa: University of Alabama Press, 2018); *Occupy Wall Street Poetry Anthology*, edited by Stephen Boyer and Filip Marinovich (New York: Occupy Wall Street, 2010); *On Rhyme*, edited by David Caplan (Liège: Presses Universitaires de Liège, 2017); *The Other Room Anthology 9*, edited by James Davies and Tom Jenks (Manchester, UK: The Other Room Press, 2017); and *Withdrawn: A Discourse*, edited by Thom Donovan and Sreshta Rit Premnath (*Shifter* 23 [2016]). My thanks to the editors and publishers.